PRAISE FOR THE LEGACY TITLES

The Legacy Titles is a must read for business owners ready to play a bigger game and take their businesses to the next level!

—**Sharon Lechter, Author of Think and Grow Rich for Women; Co-author of Rich Dad Poor Dad, Three Feet from Gold, Outwitting the Devil and many others**

This is the book to read to help grow your business and obtain an amazing quality of life. The Legacy Titles is for every business owner and entrepreneur who wants to build a real business that generates real money and has the ability to exit for real wealth.

Liza Borches, President and CEO, Carter Myers Automotive

Glenn Lundy has once again brought his special brand of magic with his new book! This book will inspire you to be great! No mediocrity if you're a fan of Glenn. He's been my friend and mentor for over 10 years, and I know his readers will 800 percent their lives and business by following his tried-and-true principles!

Lisa Copeland, Top 1% Realtor in US

Add to cart folks, ADD TO CART, and get one for all your friends! Glenn Lundy, the legend behind The Morning 5 and all things Rise & Grind, has written a masterpiece for the soul and for your guaranteed progress.

People often ask those in elevated places, if they could go back in time and advise their younger self, what would they say... well I would say to read Glenn's book, right now. This is years of hindsight for your life's foresight, a lifetime of lessons to help chart your course for success and the solid mentorship everyone needs to hear to never quit.

Glenn, you are truly one in a billion, and your Legacy Titles are just that. Thank you for taking your success and using it to give back. This is the time it is most needed and I cannot wait to see this movement in full effect. May the whole world forever understand what it's like to live life at 800%!

Danelle Delgado, "The Millionaire Maker" TeamEngage.com

I often talk about being around the right people at the right time, and Glenn Lundy is one of those people. In his new book, The Legacy Titles, he shares how leveraging 12 key principles allowed him to grow his business and, in fact, live a better life. Believe me, you will want this book in your library, and you'll come back to it time and time again.

Tim Storey, thought-leader, life strategist, author, speaker and counselor

THE LEGACY TITLES

12 PROVEN PRINCIPLES
TO SCALE YOUR BUSINESS 800%

A PARABLE FOR SUCCESS

BY GLENN LUNDY

Copyright 2024: 800 Elite Auto LLC

ISBN: 979-8-9898479-0-7

SERIES: LEGACY TITLE SERIES

PUBLISHED BY

800eliteauto, LLC

541 Darby Creek Road Suite 270

Lexington, KY 40509

Glenn@Glennlundy.com

Cover Design: Josh "x7Judy" Judy | X7Live

Publishing Services: Book Your Brand LLC | David Lloyd Strauss

To the most amazing, supportive, inspiring woman I know, and the eight beautiful children we are blessed to raise together.
Thank You.

To the most loyal, loving, determined parents I know, and the journey we went through to get to this point in life.
Thank You.

To the most incredible humans in and out of the auto industry who I have had the honor of doing life with these last five years.
Thank You.

To the five best friends I have in my life. You know who you are.
Thank You.

And lastly, to the greatest mentor, coach, leader, and friend a man could've ever asked for in life. Though things are no longer what they used to be…
Thank You.

CONTENTS

Foreword 9
Prologue 11
01. The Beginning of a Legacy 13
02. A Moment of Truth 21
03. Discovering Unexpected Treasure 27
04. Changing the Way You Start Your Day 35
05. A New Perspective 41
06. Actually Doing the Work 45
07. The Unveiling 57
08. A Rare Moment of Execution 65
09. What Do YOU Want? 73
10. There Are Diamonds Right Beneath Your Feet 83
11. Fail to Plan and You Plan to Fail 91
12. The Success Formula 105
13. Fischer Went Pee-Pee in the Potty 111
14. Seeking Opportunities to Serve 127
15. When Everything Falls Apart 137
16. Champions Attracting Champions 149
17. Books, books, and more books 165
18. Here We Go Again 179
Epilogue 191
Join the Community 193
Ready to Rise and Grind? 195

FOREWORD

For years I've always said Glenn Lundy is the most underutilized talent in America. I believe with this book, that will no longer be the case.

When Glenn gave me the final draft of "The Legacy Titles - 12 Proven Principles to Grow Your Business 800% - A Parable for Success," I was immediately struck by the profound simplicity and universal applicability of its teachings. In my journey as an entrepreneur, author, and motivational speaker, I've always emphasized the importance of core values such as gratitude, empathy, and accountability. This book not only resonates with these values, but Glenn has managed to bring them to life through practical, actionable principles.

In the fast-paced world of business and personal development, it's easy to get lost in the complexities and forget the principles that drive true success and fulfillment. "The Legacy Titles" serves as a much-needed compass, guiding readers to many fundamentals that are too often overlooked in our quest for achievement and recognition.

Each of the twelve titles in this book is a gem, providing insights that are both timeless and urgently relevant. From embracing the early hours in "The Morning 5" to understanding the profound impact of being a servant leader, the principles in this book are universal keys to unlocking not just business success, but a life of meaningful achievement and personal satisfaction.

What I particularly appreciate about this book is its approach to teaching these principles through a parable. Stories have a unique power to engage, inspire, and educate. They resonate on a level that direct advice often can't reach. By weaving these principles into a narrative, the book not only makes them more relatable but also more memorable.

As someone who has dedicated his life to empowering others to be happier, more successful, and more connected to their own values, I see "The Legacy Titles" as an invaluable resource. Whether you're an entrepreneur, a leader, a student, or just someone on a path of personal growth, the wisdom in these pages can help you build a foundation for a life filled with purpose, success, and, most importantly, happiness.

Over the years it's been incredible working with Glenn and watching him evolve and mature in both the business world, and his personal life. After you read this book, my guess is you'll be able to do the same.

Remember, the journey to success is not just about what we achieve, but who we become in the process. "The Legacy Titles" offers a roadmap for both.

— David Meltzer

PROLOGUE

Have you ever stood at the crossroads of ambition and uncertainty, wondering how to turn your grandest dreams into reality? This question haunted me as I embarked on the journey to write a book that could truly elevate the success and productivity of team leaders to levels never imagined.

For years I wasn't sure I could get this book done. For years I put together outlines, and concepts. I met with literary agents and created multiple rough drafts. I changed the theme, the topic, the title, everything. Dozens of times, if not more. For some reason it just never felt "right." The timing was always off. The principles were not quite defined enough. The book seemed practical, but at the same time I wasn't as excited about it as I thought I should be.

So, I did what I always do when I have nowhere else to turn. I prayed about it, and in prayer I was led to think about the life of Jesus and the way he shared biblical principles through parables, and how those stories he told were so memorable and impactful, that they helped completely reshape the world that we lived in.

I knew in an instant that a parable was exactly what this book needed. I began to write feverishly, and in creating a story about a middle-aged car dealer named Alfred, "The Legacy Titles" was born.

On the following pages you will find 12 Proven Principles that if applied to your business will allow you to grow 800%. This is not a guess. 800% is not a random number pulled out of thin air. It is an actual mathematical formula that has been proven not only by me personally, but by many of my clients across North America.

Now I know that for some, 800% might seem crazy. Many of you are looking to grow 5%, 15%, maybe even 25%, but 800%? That's a BIG number. Well, I assure you, continue to read along, and you'll find that not only has Alfred and his story laid out the path for you, but it's not as difficult or unachievable as you might think.

There is one caveat though. At risk of sounding cliché, the principles only work if you do. I wish I could tell you there was some magic potion that you could drink, or some "But wait there's more" gimmick that you can apply, walk away, and then, miraculously the skies part, the earth cracks open, and the riches and spoils of an 800% life come erupting from some volcano, and rain down from the sky.

But that's simply not how it works.

The results you desire will not happen overnight; however, they can happen faster than you think. There is a well-known futurist by the name of Ross Dawson that recently was quoted as saying "What used to take 2,000 years can now be done in one hundred." Do a little backwards math, and what used to take one hundred years… can now be done in five.

We've seen this in action time and time again. Names like Steve Jobs, Bill Gates, and Elon Musk have shot up to become the richest humans on earth in record time. Add in brands like Uber, Facebook, and Carvana and the pattern is seen again, and again, and again. Massive companies that are built in short order, and quickly become household names.

"What used to take 2,000 years can now be done in one hundred."

Yes Ross Dawson, I agree sir, and to think he spoke those words BEFORE they released things like ChatGPT and other AI tools that have expanded possibilities even more.

On that note, let's get into the story. One last thing though, what would life look like for you if you increased your business 800%? 800% more clients. 800% more money. 800% more impact. Don't glaze over this, really take a moment to think about what that means. 800%.

Would it change your life? Your relationships? Would it affect your health both mentally and physically? Really think about what growing 800% could do for you, and once you have that image solidified in your mind, turn the page, and let your journey to 800% begin.

CHAPTER 1
THE BEGINNING OF A LEGACY

"Every New Beginning
Comes from Another Beginnings End."
—Lucius Anneus Seneca

Alfred opened the door to his Midnight Edition Chevy Silverado for the thousandth time, a ritual that marked the beginning of another day in his life as the General Manager at Smith Chevrolet.

The birds greeted him with their melodic chirping as the sun's rays painted the eastern horizon with hues of orange and pink. There was a peculiar mix of sensations in the air—and a slight chill lingering from the fading summer, intermingled with the warm, stale embrace of the season's final days.

He climbed into the driver's seat and started the engine. The low growl of the truck was music to his ears, a familiar soundtrack to his daily commute. A faint cloud of exhaust swirled around his Maryland dealer plate, a symbol of the dealership that had been a part of his family for generations. Alfred's phone was in hand, and with a tap, he connected to the Bluetooth system. The soothing notes of the Bose stereo filled the cab with sound as he prepared for the 23-minute journey ahead.

It was September 1st, a new day, a new month. August had drawn to a close on a positive note for Smith Chevrolet. They had managed to sell 131 cars, yielding a respectable profit. The entire team was riding a wave of enthusiasm as they embraced autumn. It had been a challenging year in many respects, but their effort had propelled them to fifth position in the zone, a top-30 ranking in their region, and an above-average standing within their Chevy Dealership twenty-group. For a dealership with a 56-year legacy, they were holding their ground, but nothing out of the ordinary.

Alfred shifted his truck into drive, beginning his daily commute past rows of average-sized homes, their driveways filled with an array of different vehicles, each representing a slice of the automotive market. There were Ford Focuses, Kia Sorentos, Nissan Titans, and Toyota Tacomas, all within a few blocks of Alfred's home. A vivid red Chevy Camaro occupied the corner house, while the cul-de-sac around the corner had a fleet of mid-sized SUVs.

Every automotive brand seemed to have its presence in this neighborhood, and Alfred had no qualms about that. After all, Smith Chevrolet was more than just a Chevrolet dealership; they also sold a wide variety of used cars. What concerned Alfred, however, was the absence of his dealership's license plate frames on many of these vehicles.

A common game Alfred played, no matter where he was traveling, was to look at the license plate frames of all the cars on the road. This would tell him who the biggest dealerships were in the area. The more license plate frames, the more successful that dealership was. It was a quick and straightforward way to gauge who was winning in the area, and who wasn't.

"Smith Chevrolet" license plate frames…had unfortunately become a rare sight on the roads.

As Alfred patiently waited at a traffic light, his attention was drawn to the Toyota Corolla directly in front of him. The license plate frame read "Hav's Auto Paradise - A World of Choice." Hav's Auto Paradise was notorious in the region for its relentless advertising campaigns and predatory tactics.

Alfred's mind drifted back to the days of old, when "Smith Chevrolet" license plate frames were everywhere. In those days you couldn't drive a block without encountering the iconic silver and blue frames that proudly displayed the Smith name.

The traffic light turned green, snapping Alfred out of his trance. Just as he was about to accelerate, he got a notification on his phone. Glancing down briefly, he noticed it was an email from Doreen, his Sales Manager. It was likely another round of promotional ideas, since Doreen also helped in that capacity, and Alfred began to wonder if any of these promotions they tried would ever actually work. For years they'd tried so many different things, but oddly they seemed to always get the same results. He decided to ignore the message for now and continued on his journey to work.

As he merged onto the highway, Alfred took a deep breath, attempting to push aside his growing sense of unease. "August was a good month," he whispered to himself. His fear that others would sense his trepidation had kicked in. He couldn't afford to enter the dealership with a negative mindset; he needed to radiate positive energy and participate in the team's celebration, even if he didn't entirely feel it himself.

The noise of cars zooming past, semi-trucks shifting gears, and motorcycles weaving in and out of traffic somehow became oddly therapeutic for Alfred. Amidst the chaos, he thought to himself, "Opportunity is everywhere. Everyone buys a car."

Amidst the highway's constant movement, something unexpected caught his eye—a massive billboard stood high against the backdrop of the clear blue sky. It highlighted a sleek car with the tagline: "*Drive with history. Drive with Smith Chevrolet.*" It was an older advertisement, perhaps from a decade ago, but the sight of the billboard brought a fleeting smile to Alfred's face, and for a moment he felt a surge of pride despite his mounting concerns.

As more and more vehicles passed him, however, that glimmer of hope slowly diminished. The cars on the road might have been diverse in make and model, but their license plate frames told a consistent story— a story where Smith Chevrolet was playing an increasingly marginal role, and the competition seemed to be dominating.

Without reading the email, Alfred decided to send Doreen a quick voice text. "Hey Doreen," he began, "I've been doing some thinking. We need to strategize, and perhaps it's time for radical change. Let's set up a meeting for today."

As Alfred approached the exit ramp, making his way toward the dealership, he felt a newfound sense of determination. He was no longer satisfied with merely maintaining their current position. Something needed to change, and Alfred was beginning to feel like if he didn't take personal responsibility to make it happen, no one else would.

The remainder of his commute was spent in deep contemplation. For some odd reason, Alfred felt like something was happening. He couldn't quite put his finger on it, but it was as if this chapter of his life would need to be more than just about growing his business and selling more cars. What that looked like, he had no idea, but a lack of understanding didn't keep his mind from sensing something changing. Little did he know, in the upcoming hours, the feeling he was experiencing would reveal itself.

Alfred parked his Silverado right next to the showroom, stepped out of the truck, and was greeted by a lineup of brand-new Chevrolets, each promising potential buyers a piece of the American dream. The familiar sounds of the dealership enveloped him as he opened the door and made his way inside. Phones were ringing, salespeople could be heard negotiating deals with customers, and there was a distant rumble of car engines in the background.

Once fully inside, Alfred could tell the day was already in full swing. Doreen, a confident and dynamic woman in her mid-thirties, waved at him from her glass-walled office. Beside her, Everett, the young and tech-savvy Sales Manager/Used Car Director, was engaged in a spirited conversation with a client on speakerphone.

Alfred proceeded to his office. The wooden nameplate on his desk read "Alfred Smith, General Manager." It was a name that had graced the desks of his father and his grandfather before him, a legacy spanning three generations. He settled into his chair, and oddly, seemingly out of nowhere, he began to reflect on the weight of that legacy.

Just as he was getting deep into thought, there came a knock at the door. Doreen entered the room. "Looking forward to our meeting, Alfred. What's on your mind?"

Before Alfred could respond, his phone rang. He picked up the call with a prompt "Hello" and began listening intently. As the words flowed into his ears, a visible transformation swept over his face. He staggered backward, leaning against the wall, tears welling up, and nearly dropped to his knees—a reaction only the sudden loss of a loved one could elicit. Alfred's grandfather had passed away.

The man who started it all. The one who originally took the entrepreneurial risk, started a business, and created the opportunity for Alfred and the hundreds of others that have worked at the dealership for the last 60 years, was gone.

The words coming from the other end of the line sent Alfred's mind swirling into a tizzy of memories. For years, Alfred Smith Sr. had been Alfred's mentor. His hero. In many ways, his best friend, and now…he was gone.

The memories continued to flood his mind. Fishing with his grandfather at the cabin in Vermont. Christmases listening to his stories and sneaking cookies behind Mom's back. The time his grandfather taught him how to tie a tie, and when he had given him advice on his first prom date. The hours and hours they spent together while Alfred learned to meticulously detail a car, sell a car, appraise a car, and order more cars for their business. Alfred was devastated.

About an hour after the heart-wrenching phone call, Alfred found himself on the small balcony at the rear of the dealership. It was a place he often retreated to for moments of quiet reflection. As he gazed out at the world beyond, staring at the nearby trees, and the flocks of birds flying by, he thought about how fragile life was, and was reminded of all the things he had been taking for granted. His wife, his kids, his business; they had all become staples of his life, but if he was honest, in many ways, he had become complacent. Comfortably doing what he had always done. He was living each day as if there were some kind of guarantee there would be a tomorrow. He stood reflecting on all of this and in that moment a message from Betty, his rock, and the love of his life, interrupted his daydream.

Alfred checked his phone and saw a picture of their youngest, Lucy, covered in mud and grinning ear to ear, holding a soccer ball triumphantly. The caption read, "Scored her first goal today!" Alfred couldn't help but smile. Watching his children play sports was one of the few activities that granted Alfred time away from the demands of dealership life and connected him to the simple joys of family life. He replied with a heart emoji and added, "So proud! We'll celebrate at dinner!"

He put his phone back in his pocket, and a wave of gratitude for his wife washed over him. Betty and Alfred's love story had been ongoing for nearly twenty years now. It began during their college years and had grown into a marriage based on mutual respect and unwavering love. They had faced their share of challenges, like any couple. However, even when things seemed they were at their worst, Betty, with her unwavering faith and strength, was always able to guide Alfred, and their marriage back onto a path of values, trust, and commitment.

Suddenly, Doreen popped her head into his office. "Doing okay, Alfred?"

He managed to smile, though it felt heavy. "Just thinking about life, Doreen. Business, my family, the importance of it all— there are so many moving pieces, like some sort of complicated jigsaw puzzle. I'm just trying to put it all together, but sometimes I'm not so sure I have the full picture."

One of the things Alfred enjoyed about Doreen is they had gone through a lot together. She had been a part of Smith Chevrolet for many years now, and over time they had cultivated an enviable relationship of trust and understanding. In a way she was like a sister to him, a sister he never had growing up, but was grateful to have at this season in his life.

Doreen smirked, "And sometimes, Alfred, it may be that you've forgotten to look at the picture ON the box. Having an idea of what it's supposed to look like in the end usually helps me when I'm trying to put things together."

Alfred raised an eyebrow. "The wisdom of Doreen strikes again", he mocked.

Doreen laughed, "Remember, the puzzle always comes together. Just give it time and keep the faith. You've got this, boss."

He sighed, his doubts still lingering. "I know, Doreen. It's just... sometimes, if I'm being honest with you, I'm not always so sure what the next step is. We've come a long way as an organization, I get it, and I am grateful, but outside of buying cars, training people, and running ads, sometimes it seems like we're running in circles. I want us to blow this thing up, move it forward, reach new levels. Make the time, effort, and energy we put into this place all worth it. You know what I mean?"

Doreen stepped closer, her gaze sincere. "Alfred, doubts are natural. But remember whose name is up on that wall. What you've done so far is great, but now that's just one piece of the puzzle. It's time to think more about the future business you want to create. Oh, and for what it's worth, I believe in you."

Alfred smiled, gratitude evident in his eyes. "Thanks, Doreen. I needed that."

As the day ended, Alfred couldn't shake the profound impact of the phone call and the reflections on his personal life. Change was in the air, and he now knew this next chapter was about both growing the business and growing himself. The winds of change were beginning to blow, and Alfred was committed to navigating this new journey with courage and determination.

CHAPTER 2
A MOMENT OF TRUTH

"To Be Remembered Well by Family, Friends, and Community Is the Ultimate Career Goal."
—Gary Vaynerchuk

Five days later, Alfred stood next to his father in front of more than five hundred people. They were all dressed in black, tears pouring down many of their faces. He looked at his dad, who gave him a quiet nod, he stepped up to the microphone, and began to speak;

"Though I knew this day would one day come, I never could have imagined the son-of-a-gun would die on a Saturday! I mean, shoot, Saturdays are for selling!" Alfred exclaimed in this best rendition of his grandfather's voice he could muster. The crowd chuckled lightly, and more tears began to pour out of the crowd as they heard this long-time familiar phrase of their beloved friend.

"Saturdays are for selling...," Alfred slowly said again. This time not in the voice of his grandfather, but in the sincere and thoughtful tone of his own. "You know, 37 years ago was the first time I ever heard him say that. I remember my dad would take me over to Grandpa's house sometimes on Friday nights, and we would enjoy a meal together you know, just hang out. Then one night I asked Grandpa if I could stay the night so that he and I could watch Saturday morning cartoons together.

In his pressed shirt, always pressed, always with a tie, my grandfather looked at me in a way that made me think my question was utterly absurd. With a big smile he said, 'Saturday morning cartoons? No Alfred, Saturdays are for selling.' And for the majority of my 37 years of life, they have been.

"Whether it was me playing hide and seek with random customer's kids on Saturday mornings at the dealership, or cleaning cars in detail when we were busy. Saturdays have always been for selling. I learned to drive in the Smith Chevrolet parking lot one weekend long ago and sold my very first car there too. Even way back then, I can honestly say, for as long as I can remember, Saturdays have ALWAYS been for selling. It's been a part of every aspect of my life from the time I was born, to this very day. I mean why do you think we are having his funeral on Sunday? Because..."

"Saturdays are for selling!" the crowd replied. Everyone chuckled loudly immediately after.

"That's right. Grandpa knew that, and 56 years ago he knew that if he could start a business, and sell some cars, he could create a legacy that would make an impact on his entire family for generations to come. A legacy that would long outlast him."

The last sentence hit Alfred a little harder than he anticipated. Technically the dealership had outlasted his grandfather...by five days at this point...but would it be a legacy store that would "Long outlast him." That was now the question.

Alfred focused back on his speech.

"My grandfather believed that it all started with sales, and ended with sales, and let me tell you...he sure sold me on that idea... and many other ideas as well. That's what Grandpa did. He sold you. He sold you on the idea that you should wear a shirt and tie every day to let the world know that you mean business."

"He sold you on the idea that you needed to work your tail off, every day, no matter what, to provide for your family, your friends, your employees, and your community. He sold you on the idea that there were no limits of what's possible, that the American dream is a living, breathing entity, and should not only be trusted and tapped into, but should be explored, stretched, consistently bent and expanded at your will through sheer grit, wit, and stubborn, confounded determination!"

"Grandpa wasn't just the evidence of what was possible. He was the proof! There was no denying it. Ask his wife and she'll tell you. Ask his kids and they'll tell you too. Ask his friends at the church or his buddies at the country club. Ask the Chamber of Commerce, and the Maryland Marauders baseball, and soccer teams. Ask C.A.S.A, "Pink Navigator," and the hundreds of other non-profit organizations Al Smith and Smith Chevrolet has poured into and impacted over the last 56 years. Ask them all. I guarantee you they'll all tell you the exact same thing. Alfred Smith Sr. was a man who lived his life as an example to us all of what it means to be "sold" on an idea."

"With Al, what you saw is what you got, and what you got was a man who you knew you could stand behind. A man you could trust. A man who always practiced what he preached and wouldn't ask you to do anything he wouldn't do. He was a man of his word, and always did the right thing!

"Well at least almost always anyway. There was that one time where Grandma told him to apologize to me for eating the last piece of apple pie before I had some, and he refused, but other than that, HE ALWAYS DID THE RIGHT THING!"

The crowd was an emotional mess at this point. Alfred on the other hand, somewhat miraculously was not. He was rolling; he was in 'The Zone.' He had the audience in the palm of his hand and complete control over everything from the timing of his words, the pacing, the inflection…it was a bit crazy really. Normally when Alfred spoke, he stuttered a bit, stammered over words, and found himself constantly wondering if anyone was actually listening to him or if they just pretended to do so because he was the boss.

This time it was different; it was like he was possessed by some newfound gift of powerful speech that reminded him of…well… it reminded him of his grandpa.

"Saturdays are for selling," Alfred continued. "They sure are Grandpa, they sure are. And by God are we going to miss you. Thankfully, you did what you always do though, and made it a little easier for us to live without you physically being here. I mean between decades worth of TV commercials and that terrible little jingle you created in the basement all those years ago, something tells me we won't be able to forget you even if we wanted to. "Driving with history, yeah you're driving with history, you're driving with history, when you choose Smith Chev-ro-let!," Alfred sang.

The spirits of everyone in the room were immediately lifted as Alfred sung this timeless jingle that had been played in the area on the radio waves at least twenty times a day for the last 30 years.

"Like for real Grandpa, we get it. History matters, family-owned, long-lasting, okay, okay…. but twenty times a day?" Everyone laughed.

"History matters…" Alfred continued "History matters…history matters…His-Story matters…."

There was a long pause. The room was deathly silent as Alfred breathed out that last sentence. "His-Story matters. Grandpa lived a life that impacted all of us. Everyone in this room CHOSE to be here. Don't lose sight of that. We didn't send out any invites. You chose to be here because of the decision my grandfather, Al Smith, Sr. made all those years ago. A decision to be a man who lives life as a spotlight, shining on others and bringing out the best in them. His entire life, all ninety-three short years, this man showed up every single day for me, for my dad, for our family, and our extended families. He was always there. A rock. Never wavering. And for that I am eternally grateful. That's my grandpa's story. What's yours?"

Alfred let the pause linger this time. He knew this moment mattered. It was as though his grandfather was channeling through him to get one last message out to the people. As if from behind the wall of death, he was taking the opportunity to make a lasting impact on everyone in the room.

Alfred's voice once again changed and mimicked that of his grandfather. "Saturdays are for selling. Today is Sunday. Today is the day you get right with God. Today is the day you run with the kids, have a picnic at the park, maybe catch a football game. Today is the day where we unplug and truly take in the blessings of this thing called life." There was a long pause.

"Saturdays are for selling…and though my grandpa knew a lot, one thing he didn't know, was that last Saturday…last Saturday was HIS last Saturday. No more selling. He had punched the clock for the last time. He also didn't know he wouldn't see another Sunday.

He didn't know it was the last time he'd see his wife, or play with his great-grandkids, or enjoy that picnic at the park. He didn't know, and neither did you and I, but here's what we do know. You and me; we're the luckiest people on earth. You know why?

Because we are alive today and were actually given the choice to be here. There are many others who didn't get that luxury. Thousands, upon thousands, didn't wake up today. Grandpa no longer gets to choose, but we still do.

"So now what? You CHOSE to be here. You're listening to my voice. What choice are you going to make next? Because if all goes well, tomorrow will be Monday, this funeral will be over, and most of you will be back at work. What happens then?

"HIS-Story. Are you just gonna let them bury you, like it's just another day and move on, or are you going to choose this moment to do something MORE with your life?" The light southern accent of the 93-year-old Al Smith seemed to be getting stronger as Alfred Jr. continued. The moment was surreal, as if literally Al himself was on the mic.

"Driving with history. Notice it doesn't say anything about riding with history. Get in the driver's seat and take control of the legacy you leave in life. You've got this. I believe in you. Thank you for always believing in me."

Silence. Tears. Every eye in the room glued on Alfred.

"Let us pray." They all bowed their heads and Alfred finished with a prayer. He then turned around, walked back over to his father who was bawling profusely, handed him the mic, and walked off the stage.

CHAPTER 3
DISCOVERING UNEXPECTED TREASURE

> *"Legacy is not Leaving Something for People, it's Leaving Something in People. The Goal isn't to Live Forever; It's to Create Something that Will."*
> **—Peter Strople**

The room fell into a hush as the attorney concluded the reading of Al Smith Sr. will. It was the quiet but definitive closing of a chapter. Alfred's grandfather was officially gone.

In great detail, they had divided up parcels of land, tangible assets, liquid cash, trusts, and strategic shares of stock. Each decision was a mirror reflecting Alfred's grandfather's insight, his understanding of each recipient's needs, strengths, and potential.

The meeting up to this point had lacked surprises. Al Smith was a man whose life was an open book; he was a man of transparency and honesty. What you saw was what you got.

When all seemed to be said and done, the attorney's gaze settled on Alfred Smith III.

"Mr. Alfred Smith the III," the attorney spoke, his voice carrying subtle inflections of formality and respect.

"Yes sir," came the immediate reply, as Alfred's eyes met those of the attorney.

"Would you kindly accompany me to the adjoining room?", the legal professional requested.

"Of course," responded Alfred, curiosity starting to take over any other thoughts in his mind.

The ensuing moments unfolded in slow motion. As Alfred stepped into the private space, the attorney presented him with a package and a thumb drive.

"Before we conclude today's proceedings, your grandfather entrusted us with the task of delivering this package and video recording solely to your hands," explained the attorney. "It has been our privilege and honor to serve Mr. Al Smith's final wishes."

With a nod that served as both acknowledgment and farewell, the attorney walked out of the room, leaving Alfred alone with the package, and his increasing curiosity.

He unwrapped the package, eager with anticipation, to find an intricately carved antique wooden box.

The box was clearly from a bygone era, its wood seasoned by the passage of time. Each carving was a symbol representing the wisdom and legacy it must hold. Though technically just a box, Alfred was sure of its significance.

Then there was the thumb drive. In stark contrast to the aged wooden box, this was an indication of the digital age. Alfred was a bit surprised because his grandfather was never much for technology.

Inserting the drive into his laptop, Alfred opened the folder, and to his surprise the screen flickered, and the face of Al Smith Sr. materialized, filling the room with a presence that was as commanding as it was familiar.

Seated in his study, surrounded by books and memorabilia, the elder Smith began to speak. His voice, a sense of warmth and unyielding strength.

"Hello, Alfred," he said with a gentle smile, his eyes twinkling with the wisdom of years lived fully and deeply. "If you're watching this, it means I've left this world and it's now your turn to carry things on."

Alfred's grandfather appeared thoughtful for a moment, as if he were looking into the distance, seeing something far off and unspoken. "Life is precious, son, and it's unpredictable. It's a gift given to us for only a short while. I've had the joy of watching you grow, seeing the spark within you that's ready to catch fire. Now, it's your time."

The old man's gaze then shifted toward the mysterious box sitting beside Alfred. "You must've seen the box by now," he chuckled lightly, the sound wrapping around Alfred like a warm, comforting blanket. "It's been in our family for many generations, but it's not just a box. It holds wisdom and a legacy that I want you to have."

As Alfred watched, the screen went blurry for a moment, refocusing to reveal his grandfather's serious, contemplative face. "Inside that box are the first twelve car titles I ever had, but they're not like any other titles I've ever seen. I honestly don't know where they originally came from, but I can tell you they were given to me much the same way I'm giving them to you."

"I can also tell you that etched on the titles are twelve principles — principles that changed my life and helped me build our business. These principles were my guide, not just in building our dealership but in every venture thereafter, and now, I believe it's time for you to learn from them, to be their guardian and perhaps use them to do things far beyond anything I could've imagined."

As the elder Alfred spoke, the younger could feel a swelling pride and sadness mingling in his chest. "I'm proud of you, Alfred," his grandfather said sincerely, looking directly into the camera, and seemingly directly into Alfred's eyes.

"I've seen your dad do amazing things, and I love that man like I never knew I could love another, but you, you son are his greatest accomplishment. You have what it takes to truly make a difference as you lead and run the family business, and I am extremely confident you will."

"Goodbye, Alfred. I can only imagine how far you can go. I love you, and though I might not be able to take you fishing anymore, I will always be right here if you need me." As Alfred Smith, Sr. said those last words, he pointed to his heart.

The video ended, leaving Alfred sitting in silence. He felt comforted, and at the same time anxious as a result of what he'd just seen. His grandfather seemed to have so much more confidence in him, much more than he himself did.

He gazed back at the small chest his grandfather had alluded to, and with a sense of reverence, he opened the box. Inside, were twelve old car titles, aged and fragile, yet somehow radiating silent, inexplicable power. Laying next to them, at the bottom of the chest was one carefully sealed envelope, made of some kind of exquisite parchment paper.

He held the chest up carefully, and felt a shiver run down his spine. Inside these pieces of paper were secrets; wisdom handed down through generations. Wisdom that he now understood he was to learn, and then put into practice their timeless truths.

For a moment, Alfred sat there, holding the small chest, feeling the weight of responsibility and the whisperings of destiny circling around him. What his grandfather had built was more than just a business, more than just about selling cars. It had always been about legacy. About understanding the past to build a brighter, stronger future.

As he looked at the chest in his hands, Alfred knew that it was now his turn to embark on a journey that would determine HIS legacy, and his legacy wasn't something he planned to take lightly. He grabbed a seat at the desk next to him and leaned in to be able to see the small lettering on each title. He then slowly grabbed the carefully sealed envelope, and delicately opened it to reveal a document consisting of the most beautiful handwriting he had ever seen. He marveled over the intentionality behind each word.

The document seemed to detail an instruction manual that would guide Alfred through the proper way to consume, and execute the principles laid out on the 12 titles that were to follow. He couldn't tell by the language who had written it, but he was however clear that its origin was historic in nature, and the words on the page were written deliberately, and with intention. He leaned towards his desk and began to read:

The Legacy Titles

Legacy Titles

THE LEGACY TITLES
- 12 PRINCIPLES OF SUCCESS -

IN THE CRUCIBLE OF INDUSTRY AND INNOVATION WHERE THE SPIRIT OF INGENUITY BREATHES LIFE INTO THE INANIMATE, THERE EMERGED A CONSTELLATION OF TRUTHS, ENDURING AND UNYIELDING IN THEIR WISDOM - THE TITLES OF LEGACY. ENSHRINED WITHIN THEIR PARCHMENT ARE THE CODES, NOT MERELY TO ENDURE THE REALMS OF BUSINESS BUT TO TRIUMPH IN THE ODYSSEY OF LIFE. THEIR ORIGINS ARE AS VENERABLE AS THE ROOTS OF ANCIENT OAKS, YET THEIR TEACHINGS RESOUND WITH A VITALITY THAT COURSES THROUGH THE MODERN ARTERIES OF INDUSTRY AND INVENTION.

IT IS INCUMBENT UPON ME TO UNVEIL THE TITLES' SOLEMN PURPOSE AND THE DIVINE INTENTION WOVEN INTO THEIR FABRIC. THEY ARE LANTERNS IN THE DARKNESS, ILLUMINATING THE PATH OF THOSE WHO SEEK TO LEAVE FOOTPRINTS IN THE SANDS OF TIME, GUIDING SPIRITS TOWARDS DOMINIONS OF EXCELLENCE WHERE ORDINARY SOULS SELDOM TRAVERSE.

THESE TITLES ARE NOT MERE RELICS OF BYGONE ERAS, NOR ARE THEY THE EXCLUSIVE MANUSCRIPTS OF THE MECHANICAL REALMS. THEY TRANSCEND INDUSTRIES AND SECTORS, RESONATING WITH UNIVERSAL HARMONIES. ANCESTRAL WISDOM AND CONTEMPORARY INSIGHT BLEND WITHIN THEIR WORDS, CREATING A LEXICON OF PRINCIPLES PERPETUALLY SIGNIFICANT AND PROFOUNDLY POIGNANT.

INSTILLED WITHIN THE TITLES IS THE ESSENCE OF LEGACY, AN ODE TO THE RELENTLESS SPIRITS WHO FORGED PATHWAYS IN THE WILDERNESS OF IMPOSSIBILITY. THEY ECHO WITH THE PHILOSOPHIES THAT BRING FORWARD NOT MERELY THE MECHANICS OF CREATION BUT THE ETHOS THAT UNDERPINS ENDURING LEGACIES.

APPROACH EACH TITLE WITH A HEART OPEN TO DISCOVERY AND A MIND UNCLUTTERED BY PRECONCEPTIONS. LET EACH WORD SEEP INTO THE REALMS OF YOUR CONSCIOUSNESS, NURTURING THE SOILS OF THOUGHT AND PERSPECTIVE. READ WITH DELIBERATION, ALLOWING THE SYMPHONIES OF WISDOM TO RESONATE WITH THE MELODIES OF YOUR SPIRIT.

THE TITLES ARE TO BE EMBRACED NOT AS COMMANDS BUT AS COMPANIONS IN YOUR JOURNEY. LET THEM NOT BE CONFINED TO THE NICHES OF READING HOURS BUT LET THEIR ESSENCE PERMEATE YOUR DAYS, INFLUENCING ACTIONS, DECISIONS, AND THE MYRIAD INTERACTIONS THAT PUNCTUATE THE TAPESTRY OF EXISTENCE.

ALLOW A COMMUNION OF SOULS WITH THE TITLES. IN THEIR WISDOM, FIND REFLECTIONS OF YOUR SPIRIT AND THE ECHOES OF YOUR JOURNEY. PERMIT THEM TO BE THE MIRRORS THAT REVEAL NOT MERELY THE FEATURES OF YOUR EXTERNAL ENDEAVORS BUT THE CONTOURS OF YOUR INTERNAL LANDSCAPES.

IN THE TITLES LIES AN ODYSSEY, A VOYAGE THAT DRIVES ACROSS THE LANDS OF SELF-DISCOVERY, LEGACY BUILDING, AND THE CEASELESS QUEST FOR EXCELLENCE. IN THEIR EMBRACE, MAY YOU FIND THE ROADS THAT PROPEL YOUR LIFE TOWARDS HORIZONS WHERE THE SKIES KISS THE FRONTIERS OF POSSIBILITY AND POTENTIAL.

12 Principles of Success

In the crucible of industry and innovation where the spirit of ingenuity breathes life into the inanimate, there emerged a constellation of truths, enduring and unyielding in their wisdom — The Titles of Legacy. Enshrined within their parchment are the codes, not merely to endure the realms of business but to triumph in the odyssey of life. Their origins are as venerable as the roots of ancient oaks, yet their teachings resound with a vitality that courses through the modern arteries of industry and invention.

It is incumbent upon me to unveil the Titles' solemn purpose and the divine intention woven into their fabric. They are lanterns in the darkness, illuminating the path of those who seek to leave footprints in the sands of time, guiding spirits towards dominions of excellence where ordinary souls seldom traverse.

These Titles are not mere relics of bygone eras, nor are they the exclusive manuscripts of the mechanical realms. They transcend industries and sectors, resonating with universal harmonies. Ancestral wisdom and contemporary insight blend within their words, creating a lexicon of principles perpetually significant and profoundly poignant.

Instilled within the Titles is the essence of legacy, an ode to the relentless spirits who forged pathways in the wilderness of impossibility. They echo with the philosophies that bring forward not merely the mechanics of creation but the ethos that underpins enduring legacies.

Approach each Title with a heart open to discovery and a mind uncluttered by preconceptions. Let each word seep into the realms of your consciousness, nurturing the soils of thought and perspective. Read with deliberation, allowing the symphonies of wisdom to resonate with the melodies of your spirit.

The Titles are to be embraced not as commands but as companions in your journey. Let them not be confined to the niches of reading hours but let their essence permeate your days, influencing actions, decisions, and the myriad interactions that punctuate the tapestry of existence.

Allow a communion of souls with the Titles. In their wisdom, find reflections of your spirit and the echoes of your journey. Permit them to be the mirrors that reveal not merely the features of your external endeavors but the contours of your internal landscapes.

In the Titles lies an odyssey, a voyage that drives across the lands of self-discovery, legacy building, and the ceaseless quest for excellence. In their embrace, may you find the roads that propel your life towards horizons where the skies kiss the frontiers of possibility and potential.

Read each one to yourself and be transformed by the Legacy you create.

There was a knock on the door.

"Alfred?" It was Betty. "You okay in here honey?"

"Yeah" Alfred replied. "I'm…I'm…okay. Are you all ready to go?"

"We are all pretty tired I think; it's been quite a long day. If you're okay, I think heading home would be best." Betty nodded her head towards the exit.

Alfred stood up, sealed the parchment back in its envelope, placed it back in the chest carefully, and as he closed the lid on the titles, he took a long, deep, heavy breath. A sense of calm washed over him, and he headed to join the rest of his family in the other room.

CHAPTER 4
CHANGING THE WAY YOU START YOUR DAY

"Wisdom is the Principal Thing; Therefore, get Wisdom: and With All Thy Getting, get Understanding."
—Proverbs 4:7

The next morning, Alfred awoke filled with curiosity. A cup of coffee in hand, he headed for the shower, allowing the warm water to temporarily wash away his thoughts about the Titles. He was caught between the realms of ancient mysteries and the pressing demands of the present. Dressed and ready, he shared a brief, tender moment with Betty and the kids before stepping out, the chest filled with Titles firmly tucked under his arm.

Smith Chevrolet greeted him with its usual Monday morning stillness, the quiet hallways echoing the beginnings of a new week. Doreen was already there, a reassuring presence, adding a touch of order to the spaces. Her early arrival and gentle tidying up brought a subtle warmth to the place.

In the solitude of his office, and feeling the pull of the Titles, Alfred decided it was time to delve into their mysteries. With the approach of the day offering a gentle pause, he opened the chest and allowed himself to be drawn into the pages, beginning with the Title Marked I.

Title I

— CERTIFICATE OF TITLE NUMBER I —

— THE MORNING 5 —
ARISE EARLY AND BE A CREATOR

LISTEN, YOU DILIGENT PURSUER OF SUCCESS AND FULFILLMENT, TO THE TITLE MARKED I, WHICH SOFTLY WHISPERS THE DAWN'S MELODY: "THE MORNING 5 - ARISE EARLY AND BE A CREATOR." THIS ANCIENT WISDOM UNFOLDS LIKE THE FIRST LIGHT OF DAY, ILLUMINATING THE PATH OF THE STEADFAST WITH ITS GENTLE GLOW, OFFERING CLARITY AND VISION TO THOSE WHO HEED ITS CALL.

FIRST, I SHALL ENGRAVE THE SACRED DECREE UPON MY HEART: "NEVER YIELD TO THE DESIRES OF SLUMBER." WITH THE MORNING'S CALL, AS THE ROOSTER PROCLAIMS THE DAWN, I SHALL RISE, SWIFT AND DETERMINED. TO RISE THEN LAY AGAIN IS THE TEMPTRESS OF INDOLENCE, SEEKING TO DRAG ME INTO THE ABYSS OF WASTED HOURS AND MISSED OPPORTUNITIES. I SHALL NOT HEED ITS BEGUILING CALL BUT SHALL SPRING FORTH, READY TO EMBRACE THE RICHNESS OF A NEW DAY WITH OPEN ARMS AND A VIGILANT SPIRIT.

SECOND, IN THE PRECIOUS SOLITUDE OF DAWN, COMMUNICATION WITH OTHERS SHALL NOT DICTATE MY ACTIONS. THE ENCHANTING DESIRE TO, AND CEASELESS BECKONING OF, THE WORLD SHALL HOLD NO SWAY OVER MY SACRED MORNING RITUALS. THESE INITIAL, PRECIOUS MOMENTS OF THE DAY ARE MINE ALONE-NOT FOR GOSSIPING WITH THE NEIGHBORS, NOT FOR DROWNING IN ENDLESS NEWSLETTERS, NOT FOR THE EXTERNAL VOICES CLAMORING FOR MY ATTENTION. IN THE TRANQUIL STILLNESS OF DAWN, I SHALL RECLAIM MY TIME, MY FOCUS, AND MY PEACE.

THIRD, AS THE INK OF NIGHT FADES, REVEALING THE CANVAS OF DAY, I SHALL TAKE PEN IN HAND AND WRITE, INSCRIBING MY GRATITUDE AND ASPIRATIONS UPON THE PARCHMENT OF MY SOUL. WITH A HEART OVERFLOWING WITH THANKS FOR LIFE'S BLESSINGS, BOTH GRAND AND HUMBLE, I SHALL ALSO OUTLINE MY AMBITIONS, SKETCHING A ROADMAP FOR THE JOURNEY AHEAD, GUIDED BY THE NORTH STAR OF MY DEEPEST AND MOST CHERISHED DREAMS.

FOURTH, THE DAWN IS A SYMPHONY OF RENEWAL, A CHORUS OF LIFE AND VITALITY ECHOING THROUGHOUT THE COSMOS. I SHALL JOIN THIS DIVINE ORCHESTRA, TENDING TO MY PHYSICAL VESSEL WITH DELIBERATE, AFFECTIONATE CARE. THROUGH EXERCISES THAT INVIGORATE AND STRENGTHEN, THROUGH PRACTICES THAT HEAL AND REJUVENATE, I SHALL PREPARE MY BODY FOR THE ADVENTURES AND CHALLENGES THAT AWAIT WITH THE RISING SUN, FORTIFYING MYSELF WITH VIGOR AND ENDURANCE.

LASTLY, AS THE FIRST RAYS OF SUNLIGHT GENTLY CARESS THE EARTH, STIRRING IT FROM SLUMBER, I SHALL SEND FORTH AN ENCOURAGING MESSAGE, A BEACON OF HOPE AND INSPIRATION, TO MY FELLOW TRAVELERS ON THIS JOURNEY OF LIFE. LIKE MORNING DEW THAT NOURISHES THE FLOWER, MY WORDS SHALL OFFER SUPPORT AND UPLIFT THE SPIRITS OF THOSE AROUND ME, FOSTERING AN ATMOSPHERE OF CAMARADERIE AND MUTUAL ASSISTANCE.

THEREFORE, WITH THE HERALDING OF EACH DAWN, LET ME FAITHFULLY OBSERVE THESE SACRED RITES, THE MORNING 5, FOR WITHIN THEM RESIDES THE SECRET TO A LIFE OF CREATION AND FULFILLMENT. WITH THE FIRST LIGHT OF DAY AS MY ALLY, I SHALL BE A CREATOR, A WEAVER OF POSSIBILITIES, A DREAMER OF DREAMS. LET THE MORNING, WITH ITS PROMISE AND POTENTIAL, BE MY CANVAS, AND LET ME PAINT UPON IT WITH THE VIBRANT HUES OF HOPE, ACTION, AND UNWAVERING PURSUIT OF GREATNESS. THUS, SHALL I LIVE; THUS, SHALL I THRIVE. FOR IN THE SACRED HOURS OF DAWN, I SHALL DISCOVER THE KEYS TO UNLOCK THE TREASURE TROVE OF A LIFE WELL-LIVED AND A LEGACY WELL-CRAFTED.

The Title Marked I

— The Morning 5 —
Arise Early and Be a Creator."

Listen, diligent pursuer of success and fulfillment, to the Title Marked I, which softly whispers the dawn's melody: "The Morning 5 – Arise Early and Be a Creator." This ancient wisdom unfolds like the first light of day, illuminating the path of the steadfast with its gentle glow, offering clarity and vision to those who heed its call.

First, I shall engrave the sacred decree upon my heart: "Never yield to the desires of slumber." With the morning's call, as the rooster proclaims the dawn, I shall rise, swift and determined. To rise then lay again is the temptress of indolence, seeking to drag me into the abyss of wasted hours and missed opportunities. I shall not heed its beguiling call but shall spring forth, ready to embrace the richness of a new day with open arms and a vigilant spirit.

Second, in the precious solitude of dawn, communication with others shall not dictate my actions. The enchanting desire to, and ceaseless beckoning of, the world shall hold no sway over my sacred morning rituals. These initial, precious moments of the day are mine alone—not for gossiping with the neighbors, not for drowning in endless newsletters, not for the external voices clamoring for my attention. In the tranquil stillness of dawn, I shall reclaim my time, my focus, and my peace.

Third, as the ink of night fades, revealing the canvas of day, I shall take pen in hand and write, inscribing my gratitude and aspirations upon the parchment of my soul. With a heart overflowing with thanks for life's blessings, both grand and humble, I shall also outline my ambitions, sketching a roadmap for the journey ahead, guided by the North Star of my deepest and most cherished dreams.

Fourth, the dawn is a symphony of renewal, a chorus of life and vitality echoing throughout the cosmos. I shall join this divine orchestra, tending to my physical vessel with deliberate, affectionate care. Through exercises that invigorate and strengthen, through practices that heal and rejuvenate, I shall prepare my body for the adventures and challenges that await with the rising sun, fortifying myself with vigor and endurance.

Lastly, as the first rays of sunlight gently caress the earth, stirring it from slumber, I shall send forth an encouraging message, a beacon of hope and inspiration, to my fellow travelers on this journey of life. Like morning dew that nourishes the flower, my words shall offer support and uplift the spirits of those around me, fostering an atmosphere of camaraderie and mutual assistance.

Therefore, with the heralding of each dawn, let me faithfully observe these sacred rites, the Morning 5, for within them resides the secret to a life of creation and fulfillment. With the first light of day as my ally, I shall be a creator, a weaver of possibilities, a dreamer of dreams. Let the morning, with its promise and potential, be my canvas, and let me paint upon it with the vibrant hues of hope, action, and unwavering pursuit of greatness. Thus, shall I live; thus, shall I thrive. For in the sacred hours of dawn, I shall discover the keys to unlock the treasure trove of a life well-lived and a legacy well-crafted.

"Really?" thought Alfred. Another thing telling me I must "Get up early! Beat the sun! Attack the day! Ugh!" He'd heard this his entire adult life but didn't anyone understand he was a "night owl" not an "early bird". I mean come on! Not everyone can be a morning person, can they?

Alfred chuckled to himself. He knew he was just making excuses, but seriously, these Titles had to be at least one hundred years old, and the idea of getting up early, and having a disciplined morning routine still resounded. He knew he was going to have a challenging time attacking this one head on but was grateful the Title broke down each step so eloquently.

He started reading the next Title when Doreen popped her head in.

"You got a second Alfred?" she questioned.

Alfred tucked the Titles back in the chest and put them in his desk.

"Of course," Alfred said, as he stood up and headed towards the doorway.

Together they walked down the hall and into the showroom where they began conversing and strategizing about the day ahead.

While doing so, Alfred noticed some salespeople starting to trickle in. There was Jean Paul and Kevin who both looked like they'd had a long night, and then in a rush, John Allen came through the door. A few minutes went by, and then came Tustin, followed by Patrick. They seemed jovial enough and Alfred could hear them saying something about grabbing some breakfast.

One by one they meandered into the showroom and over to their individual offices. Matt and Stacy, Melissa, and Michelle; they each made their way in, most of them drinking some sort of energy drink and taking a slow approach to their day.

Now that Alfred had read the Title Marked One, he couldn't help but think about the striking difference between the intentionality of "The Morning 5" and the current state of his business. In all fairness, Smith Chevrolet was lucky if they got any kind of production before 11:00 A.M. Between all the gossiping, breakfast burritos, doughnuts, and energy drink runs, not much actual work got done in the mornings. It was quite a stark revelation, but now incredibly easy to see. How he'd never noticed it before was beyond him.

The rest of the day was a blur. Alfred went through his normal routine of managing the day-to-day operations, running reports, handling issues, searching for keys, planning his marketing, etc.

It wasn't long before the sun began to set, and the members of the Smith Chevrolet team began going through their closing rituals. After all was locked up, Afred hopped in his truck and headed home.

CHAPTER 5
A NEW PERSPECTIVE

> *"Everyone Thinks of Changing the World,*
> *but No One Thinks of Changing Themselves."*
> **—Leo Tolstoy**

Later that night, Alfred sat down and read each of the Titles in the chest carefully. There were twelve in all, each with profound wisdom inked intently on their ragged and tattered pages.

Before him had unfolded a veritable blueprint of success and fulfillment—a meticulously detailed map breaking down the path to an invincible fortress of wealth and influence. Each word was a steppingstone; every principle, a key to unlocking the gates of success.

Once complete, Alfred reclined into his chair and inhaled deeply, resting in a moment of profound contemplation. He could feel the cool air fill his lungs for what seemed like the first significant breath in a long, long time. It was as though he had been submerged, lost in the oceanic depths of the ancient wisdom within the Titles, forgetting to breathe, and drowning in the enchanting allure of the words etched into their pages.

Suddenly the appearance of Alfred's revered grandfather seemed to materialize in his mind. It was as if he could perceive the very essence of him pulsating beside him, his spirit immortalized and brought back to life through the Titles.

The late Al Smith Sr.'s life could only be described as one of service and humility. He was the epitome of a servant leader, just as the Title Marked Seven had described.

His demeanor was magnetic, attracting respect not through arrogant demands but through a quiet, unassuming strength that pulled people into his orbit, pointing towards the words etched on the Title Marked Eleven.

Al had always had a hypnotic quality to his presence; a subtle enchantment that made you feel special and important, as though, in that moment, you were the center of everything, and the world revolved around you. Alfred realized this was the result of the Title Marked Five.

Al had also been an avid reader, a man who not only devoured books but shared their wisdom generously with those around him, often distributing them from a stash he kept conveniently tucked behind his desk. His love for knowledge wasn't a selfish pursuit; it was an exercise for everyone, shared liberally with anyone in need. Clearly this pointed to the Title Marked Ten.

As Alfred continued to reflect, he began to think about how he had found himself confounded by the meticulously designed systems that his grandfather had established when it came to the operations of their dealership. It always seemed as though there was some complex magic machine with cogs and wheels that worked diligently under his grandfather's skilled hands. However, the fog of confusion lifted after Alfred read the Title Marked Four that broke down an extremely specific formula for both sales and scale.

He could see the patterns now, the exquisite tapestry of principles and values woven meticulously in the Titles, and then lived outwardly by his grandfather. Each thread a testament to his unwavering commitment to the principles enshrined in the Titles.

In stark contrast, Alfred himself was a blank canvas, untouched by the discipline and wisdom that painted his grandfather's life portrait.

He was not a morning person. His mornings were rushed affairs, beginning with the grinding sound of the alarm, and ending with him dashing through the doors of the dealership, barely making it in time. His approach to life and work was markedly different, often advising others to leave their personal lives at the door.

Books? Alfred had not opened many, let alone gained their knowledge or shared their wisdom. In many ways, he was navigating through a storm without a compass, caught in a cycle of lack luster motivation and enduring tiredness, going back and forth between periods of frantic action and painful burnout.

However, as he held the Titles, a strange sensation washed over him; a tidal wave of energy and determination infusing his veins with newfound purpose. He had mentors before, seasoned guides who attempted to steer him through the terrains of life, but none wielded the transformative power pulsating within the Titles.

This moment marked a transition from the beaten path, a season of metamorphosis. Armed with the ancestral wisdom within the parchment, Alfred felt ready, perhaps for the first time in his life, to embrace change with open arms.

CHAPTER 6
ACTUALLY DOING THE WORK

*"The Sun Has Not Caught Me
in Bed in 50 Years."*
—**Thomas Jefferson**

Alfred prepared to attack the first Title, considering the current routine for both him and his dealership consisted of starting late, a whole lot of energy drinks, and an unmeasurable amount of wasted time mixed with lackluster production, he knew this was not going to be easy. To ensure he understood it, Alfred read the Title one more time:

The Morning 5 — Arise Early and Be a Creator

Listen, diligent pursuer of success and fulfillment, to the Title Marked I, which softly whispers the dawn's melody: "The Morning 5 – Arise Early and Be a Creator." This ancient wisdom unfolds like the first light of day, illuminating the path of the steadfast with its gentle glow, offering clarity and vision to those who heed its call.

First, I shall engrave the sacred decree upon my heart: "Never yield to the desires of slumber." With the morning's call, as the rooster proclaims the dawn, I shall rise, swift and determined. To rise then lay again is the temptress of indolence, seeking to drag me into the abyss of wasted hours and missed opportunities. I shall not heed its beguiling call but shall spring forth, ready to embrace the richness of a new day with open arms and a vigilant spirit.

Second, in the precious solitude of dawn, communication with others shall not dictate my actions. The enchanting desire to and ceaseless beckoning of the world shall hold no sway over my sacred morning rituals. These initial, precious moments of the day are mine alone—not for gossiping with the neighbors, not for drowning in endless newsletters, not for the external voices clamoring for my attention. In the tranquil stillness of dawn, I shall reclaim my time, my focus, and my peace.

Third, as the ink of night fades, revealing the canvas of day, I shall take pen in hand and write, inscribing my gratitude and aspirations upon the parchment of my soul. With a heart overflowing with thanks for life's blessings, both grand and humble, I shall also outline my ambitions, sketching a roadmap for the journey ahead, guided by the North Star of my Deepest and most cherished dreams.

Fourth, the dawn is a symphony of renewal, a chorus of life and vitality echoing throughout the cosmos. I shall join this divine orchestra, tending to my physical vessel with deliberate, affectionate care. Through exercises that invigorate and strengthen, through practices that heal and rejuvenate, I shall prepare my body for the adventures and challenges that await with the rising sun, fortifying myself with vigor and endurance.

Lastly, as the first rays of sunlight gently caress the earth, stirring it from slumber, I shall send forth an encouraging message, a beacon of hope and inspiration, to my fellow travelers on this journey of life. Like morning dew that nourishes the flower, my words shall offer support and uplift the spirits of those around me, fostering an atmosphere of camaraderie and mutual assistance.

Therefore, with the heralding of each dawn, let me faithfully observe these sacred rites, the Morning 5, for within them resides the secret to a life of creation and fulfillment. With the first light of day as my ally, I shall be a creator, a weaver of possibilities, a dreamer of dreams. Let the morning, with its promise and potential, be my canvas, and let me paint upon it with the vibrant hues of hope, action, and unwavering pursuit of greatness. Thus, shall I live; thus, shall I thrive. For in the sacred hours of dawn, I shall discover the keys to unlock the treasure trove of a life well-lived and a legacy well-crafted.

Okay, so obviously the Titles were written in a different time period and needed a little modern-day interpretation. Alfred went through each step and wrote himself a note he could easily refer to.

STEP 1. NO SNOOZE BUTTON. WAKE UP AND GET YOUR BUTT UP.

STEP 2. NO PHONE FIRST THING IN THE MORNING. (SAME AS NEWLETTERS AND WHATNOT.)

STEP 3. GRATITUDE AND GOALS. WRITE THEM DOWN.

STEP 4. TAKE CARE OF THE PHYSICAL. EXERCISE DAILY.

STEP 5. SEND OUT AN ENCOURAGING MESSAGE. TEXT, DM, STICKY NOTE, WHATEVER.

As he stared at the note, he faintly remembered that his grandfather used to model this morning routine exactly. Always up before the sun and writing in his journal before going for a light run, or in his older age, a brisk walk. The more Alfred thought about it, he could also recall getting random messages of encouragement from his grandfather every few months or so.

His mind then wandered to the dealership. He remembered when he was young that his grandfather would have team meetings every single day. They were always high energy, and informational, and it seemed like his people were excited to attend. Now with the Title in hand, he was going to implement The Morning 5 for himself, but also change the way they started their day at work as well.

When the alarm clock rang the next morning, Alfred reluctantly turned it off and slid out of bed. He was tired, but not devastatingly so, and as he habitually reached out to grab his phone, he was immediately reminded of one line of the Title Marked One that stated, "Do not allow others into your mind."

Though written in a time before cell phones, clearly jumping onto his phone would contradict the Title. Social media feeds, emails, text messages, news updates, ALL fall in the category of allowing others into your mind. In fact, they're ALL designed to do exactly that. "No phone first thing in the morning," Thought Alfred. "Got it."

He made his way to the kitchen, stumbling a bit through the myriad of shoes, toys, and other obstacles along the way. He grabbed a tall glass, filled it with ice, and poured himself some water. He then shuffled to his home office, grabbed a pen and paper, and began to write.

"I am thankful for...." He paused for a moment. So much to be thankful for and yet in this moment, his mind drew a blank.

I am thankful for…my wife, he wrote.

I am thankful for my kids, he continued.

I am thankful for my house, he penned.

And over a period of about ten minutes Alfred found he was able to write down ten things he was thankful for. He then moved on to the next step: Goals.

I am going to follow through on the Titles. He beamed, proud of himself for thinking of this first.

I am going to be the number one dealer in the zone. He wrote firmly. This time he noticed a tinge of hesitation. Self-doubt began to kick in, but Alfred continued.

I am going to invest time and energy not just at work, but with my family. This was a big one. For years, Alfred had been the first one in and the last one out at his dealership. He would typically arrive early each day and get home often after nine or ten o'clock P.M.

He began to write down several more goals, and once he was done, he set the pen down and read through the list.

Satisfied with his accomplishment and energized by the process, he then made his way to the Peloton bike that had been sitting in the basement collecting dust for years. He strapped on his red and black rigid, plastic clip in shoes, pulled up a Kendall Toole workout, and started to pedal. It wasn't pretty and, in the end, he was pouring sweat head to toe, but he finished. Grabbing a towel to wipe the sweat dripping down his face, he made his way upstairs to complete the last step of his "Morning 5."

Alfred's kids were sleeping. He slowly crept into each of their rooms and whispered in their ears. "You are beautiful, you are wonderful, and you are loved." Lucy was the last one he visited, and as he turned to walk away, she opened her eyes slightly and a smile crept across her face. "Love you daddy," she sweetly and softly proclaimed. Alfred's heart melted as he watched her beautiful eyes close and drift back to sleep.

He continued with his morning and was genuinely surprised at how much energy he had, even though he had woken up significantly earlier than usual. He felt as though he had tapped into some sort of weird vibration or something where his mind was sharp, his body felt rejuvenated, and his vigor revitalized. In short, he felt great.

He went through the ritual of taking a shower, grabbing some breakfast, helping a bit with the kids, and then headed for work. This time, unlike past commutes, instead of focusing on the lack of license plate frames in the area, he focused on how he could get his dealership to also change the way they started their day.

He arrived at the dealership, sat down, and mapped out the framework for a morning meeting. It was still well before 8:30 A.M. and he wanted the team to do things a little bit differently today. He sat down and began to script what the meeting needed to look like. Drawing a blank initially, he was soon reminded of an acronym his grandfather had once taught him.

"L.E.A.D.D." He could almost hear his grandfather saying. "Listen. Encourage. Advise. Develop. Daily."

His grandfather would teach that this was the key to effective leadership. Following this process would always allow for a deeper connection in relationships, with clients, employees, kids, your spouse, whomever, and it also allowed you to get way more out of those you were responsible for leading. Anyone and everyone would respond well to this cadence.

The memory began to flood back to him, "The process is simple." His grandfather would say, "Start every conversation by remembering the philosophy *Two ears, one **mouth and listen twice as much as you speak**.* Every conversation you have, make sure to begin with the intention of listening to what the other person has to say. Then, as the conversation continues, ask a lot of questions. This will help you create additional opportunities for them to speak. All the while listening intently and gaining a clear understanding of what they're saying."

How Alfred had forgotten all of this was beyond him, but suddenly he could remember his grandfather's words of wisdom, as if they had just been spoken to him yesterday.

"After you've listened to them," Al continued. "You can now respond with words of encouragement. Even if you don't necessarily agree with what you've just heard, it's important that you find something about them that you can highlight, compliment, or praise them for. **Always remember that everyone has something great in them, and it's your job as a leader to identify what that is and draw it out.**"

"The next step is to advise," Al taught. "This is where you take the time to share with the employee, the potential client, the spouse or the child, areas of growth for them. This could be things they aren't doing properly, or problems that have arisen, solutions you can share, anything like that. The key to advising people is making sure to remember the famous quote *To be kind is to be clear, and if you're going to error on one side or the other, error on the side of clear.* Always make sure when you advise others you do so in a kind way. A way that makes truly clear the issue, and the expectations going forward."

"Then there is the "Development" piece. This can be summed up as simply making sure that whomever you are talking to or leading, walks away knowing something they did not know at the beginning of the conversation, phone call, or meeting."

The unexpected memory caused Alfred to think about how he could introduce this in his morning meetings. If he could execute the L.E.A.D.D. formula correctly, with a little bit of tinkering to make it fit, he might just have an outline for meetings that he could not only use himself, but potentially share with others. He grabbed a pen and paper and began to jot down some notes.

Listen – **In order to do this, I must be the first one in the room so that I can hear what my team is talking about.** Were they up late last night playing Fortnite? Does anyone have a family member that is sick, or passed away? Is there a birthday coming up, or any other event of significance? All these things can be discovered if I am the first one in the room, and once I know what matters to them, I can more effectively connect with the team.

Also, I need to activate their energy levels through sound. No one wants to walk into a room that feels sterile or empty. Putting music on the speakers solves this, but it must be the right music. Music with no words, (as the Title Marked One states no "Outside Voices"), that can sway or trigger them in any way first thing in the morning. Also, it must be music that is upbeat and positive. No hardcore rap, or heavy metal, no slow country music, or ballads. High energy, instrumental music is the key.

Encourage – Once the official meeting time arrives, every meeting needs to start by encouraging the behaviors I want to see more of. If we need more Google reviews, then put positive reviews up on the screen, read them aloud in front of the team, and celebrate the person who received it. The same can be done if we are chasing a production target, or doing some sort of social media challenge, etc. Whatever it is we want to see more of, we celebrate. **And no boring golf claps. We get loud, we get wild, and we truly energize those that are being highlighted.**

Odd as it sounds, thinking about this reminded Alfred of how they had potty-trained Lucy. Every time she went to the bathroom properly, he, his wife, and his other two kids would line up outside the bathroom. Lucy would get three Skittles as a reward, and then the whole family would cheer and dance singing a silly song. "Lucy went pee-pee in the potty! Lucy went pee-pee in the potty! Lucy went pee-pee in the potty! Because she's a really big girl!" Every time they did this Lucy would get the biggest smile on her face, and in time she was fully potty-trained.

In a roundabout way this was the same strategy Alfred was going to implement in the meetings. They were going to ridiculously celebrate and encourage the behaviors they wanted to see more of. It worked on three-year-olds, and oddly enough, the Titles hinted to the fact that it would work with adults too.

Advise – This is the point in the meeting where we will share any issues or problems we need to resolve. Maybe it's that people have been showing up late, and we simply can't have that anymore. Maybe it's that the paperwork isn't getting properly filled out. The business isn't being treated properly or people are leaving trash lying around. Maybe there are consistent customer issues, low performance, or anything else that needs direct attention. **The premise is that once you've LISTENED to your people, and then you've ENCOURAGED your people, you've now EARNED the right to ADVISE your people**. Most managers start, (and end), with the ADVISE piece and wonder why no one responds to them. Leaders understand that we must touch someone's heart before we can ask for a hand and following the L.E.A.D.D. process does exactly that.

Develop – The premise here is that we must make sure the team walks out of the room knowing at least one thing they didn't know when they walked in. It is also important to note that we should NEVER ask anyone to do anything, and then not take the time to teach them how to do it. As leaders, we are responsible to not only guide, navigate, and direct, but also to educate, nurture, and truly develop the skills necessary for our people to be successful.

Alfred thought through this, and quickly identified that his people had been struggling to overcome common objections for a while now. Considering they were not training daily; it was now clear why that was the case. He continued to write it out:

Each daily meeting is to be tied to a bigger concept. Each concept is tied to at least a week of development. Each weekly development piece is tied to a bigger monthly, quarterly, or annual concept. In the end it is all tied to an infinitely expanding successful career.

For example, the skill we want to develop is:

"How to handle common objections properly."

The weekly theme will be the objection where the customer says, "I need to think about it."

The daily development will be ten minutes of role-play.

The following week, the skill we want to develop is still:

"How to handle common objections properly."

The weekly theme will be the objection, "Price is too high."

The daily development will be ten minutes of role-play.

Over a period of 3 months, 6 months, or 12 months, counting to infinity, our people continue to grow and home in their skills. What we are teaching is not as important as understanding that your people MUST walk away knowing something new in which they didn't know walking in. Without this piece your meetings will become repetitive and ineffective.

And then regarding the last "D" in L.E.A.D.D.

Daily- The last and final piece of the puzzle. The L.E.A.D.D. process only truly shows its incredible power when used every single day, and the same is true for the morning meeting. **It doesn't matter if it's two people or two thousand, there is a compound effect that happens only over time which makes it effective. You won't see it at first, but in time, it will blow your mind.**

As Alfred was concluding the morning meeting outline, he was reminded of a video he had seen by the great Les Brown, one of the most notable motivational speakers in the world. In the video, Les told a story about a bamboo tree, and the spectacular way in which it grows:

"A Chinese bamboo tree takes five years to grow. It has to be watered and fertilized in the ground where it has been planted every day. It doesn't break through the ground for five years. After five years, once it breaks through the ground, it will grow ninety feet tall in five weeks! The question is, did the Chinese bamboo tree grow ninety feet tall in five weeks or in five years? The answer is obvious. It grows ninety feet tall in five years. If at any time that person stopped watering and fertilizing that tree, it would die in the ground. Some people do not have the patience to wait for the tree to grow, yet many people do."

Always remember the story of the bamboo tree. Its seed must be watered every day for five years before it ever sprouts and breaks ground, however, once it breaks ground, it will grow 90 ft in a matter of weeks. This is the power of a daily routine in our lives; the dividends it pays are far beyond our wildest expectations."

This was it. Listen, Encourage, Advise, and Develop, and do it Daily. That was all Alfred needed to do in order to change the way the business started its day. It wasn't rocket science, just an intentional start that would put him and the team in a position of productivity first thing in the morning.

He messaged Doreen and told her to make sure the whole team was in the meeting room at 8:30 am. He had something new to share with all of them.

CHAPTER 7
THE UNVEILING

> *"Coming together is a beginning,*
> *staying together is progress,*
> *and working together is success."*
> **—Henry Ford**

Alfred went up to the meeting room, connected his laptop, and searched YouTube for "motivational upbeat instrumental music," in hopes of finding the perfect music for the morning. He was surprised to see thousands of hours of such music existed. He then scrolled through until he found a song that he thought matched the energy and tone for which he was hoping. He pressed play, turned up the volume, and like magic, the meeting room came to life.

He then waited, and as the minutes ticked by, his team started to trickle in. One by one they meandered into the meeting room as Alfred watched the surprised smiles on their faces. "What's this all about?" one of his salespeople asked. Meanwhile, another started dancing as she came in, and a third stepped in looking around curiously, before he started handing out high-fives.

As more members of the team arrived, Alfred began to walk around the room giving people fist bumps and asking how each of them were doing. Some responded blandly, others with enthusiasm, but no matter how they reacted, they all seemed to appreciate the interaction.

Alfred continued asking questions like: "How was your night?" "How are you feeling this morning?" "Have you been working out?" "How is your daughter doing?" "Are you investing your money like I told you? "All questions that were designed to let THEM do the talking, while also learning more about what's going on in their life.

As the conversations continued, Alfred was pleasantly surprised at how much they had to say, and even more surprised to find out how much he didn't know about them. He made sure to jot down a few notes on his reMarkable tablet once he got back to the front of the room and vowed to prioritize getting to know his people better moving forward.

A little after 8:30 A.M. the meeting began. Alfred had wanted to start on time, but because he had sprung the meeting on the team last minute, he knew some of them would be late, and as he anticipated, they were indeed.

No harm, no foul though, it was day one, and if they just stayed consistent with DAILY morning meetings, he was sure that in time it wouldn't be an issue.

Once everyone was settled, Alfred let out a resounding "Good morning, good morning, good morning," to which a chatter of "good mornings" came back from his team.

"I want to start by recognizing some of you for a job well done. As you all know, Google reviews are an incredibly important part of our success here at Smith Chevrolet and some of you have been doing a phenomenal job with it."

Alfred then projected a recent Google review onto the screen that he had collected earlier that morning. He then read the Google review aloud:

5 Out of 5 stars

Google

Kerry T. Johnson
December 20, 2023

I'm very pleased with my experience dealing with the dealership. I ordered a new Corvette and the experience was seamless. The Corvette came in this past Tuesday and we drove down from Indiana to take delivery today. We will actually have it shipped from the dealer Wednesday 9/20 using one of their recommended shippers. James the gentleman that will be delivering my vehicle has been excellent to talk to and very knowledgeable. The attached picture is the vehicle parked inside where it will stay until shipped as my sales person knew how picky I was and guaranteed me that it would be kept safe until it ships, which I really appreciated. I want to give a big shout out to my sales person Jason Carroll, one of the most knowledgeable sales person that you will find on Corvettes. He has been excellent to work with. I could've bought my Corvette from any dealership in Indiana but he is the reason I bought from a dealership in Maryland. I look forward to my car being delivered to my home on Wednesday.

Update 9/8
my Corvette was delivered today, as promised in perfect condition as it was on Saturday when I inspected it. I can't say enough about James, who delivered the car and his professionalism and his attention, to detail to making sure every was perfect. I would highly recommend him if you want a vehicle shipped the best Shipper I've ever dealt with. And I can't say enough about Jason Carroll our sales person. Everything he told me he would do he delivered on. If you're looking for a Corvette or any vehicle, I would highly recommend him, one of the top sales people I've dealt with and I've had many exotic cars.

Smith Chevrolet is lucky to have two top-notch people like James and Jason they are five star when it comes to customer satisfaction.

The team erupted with applause as Jason stood up and took multiple bows. Alfred was immediately blown away at the interaction. He then moved to the next review.

5 Out of 5 stars
Google

Brandon Randolph
November 15, 2024

Taking the advice from my Step Father, I drove from Louisville Kentucky and walk in with my mother to meet Liza Borches my car salesperson at Smith Chevrolet. The experience and personal relationship in the moment was far more than expected. I had the honor to meet Liza and to buy a truck with confidence from a well respected dealership.

I could write about the whole experience, but to keep it brief... I walked in thinking I'd be attacked and what I got was a Saleswoman of honor, respectful and she treated my mother with respect. Smith Chevrolet should be proud to have Liza Borches as an employee.

**Thank you for the experience and the music you play.
God bless.**

Another eruption of applause, and instead of getting up and bowing, Liza sat humbly while the teammates next to her patted her encouragingly on the shoulders. She was blushing a bit, but you could tell she was loving the moment.

Alfred went on to read two more reviews, and then took time to highlight some other team members for their performance. "Congrats to Jessica for her two cars sold yesterday!" Everyone clapped and cheered. "And also, Nick and Alex both got perfect surveys yesterday, great job you two!" Again, a round of applause.

"And lastly, Kacey who went out of her way Sunday to make sure one of our customers didn't have to miss her daughter's birthday party. Kacey actually drove over to meet the woman in a Walmart parking lot, after hearing she was stranded and her car wouldn't start. With her bike literally in the back of her truck, she drove over, met with the woman, pulled her bike out of the back of the truck, gave the lady her truck, and then proceeded to ride her bike back home!"

"Kacey then had the customers vehicle towed to the dealership, made sure they made it a priority, and then after it was fixed, she delivered it back to the woman and got her truck back! Can you believe it? Thank you for going out of your way Kacey! That's what I'm talking about!"

This time the room absolutely exploded with cheers! They were so loud, people across the parking lot heard their roar. The energy in the room was absolutely electric at this point, and all Alfred could think was that if it weren't for the morning meeting, none of Kacey's peers would've ever even known it happened. She maybe would've gotten a "good job" or two, but that would've been the extent of it. Instead, now everyone was cheering Kacey's name as she blushed vibrantly, while smiling ear to ear.

It was one of those moments Alfred immediately knew he would never forget.

Alfred did a quick audit. He had completed the "L" in L.E.A.D.D. and now with the celebrations the "E" was complete. Next it was time for the "A." It was time to "Advise."

"Alright guys, listen up. This morning I walked through the lot and found multiple cars unlocked. There was also a pile of cigarette butts by the customer side entrance, and that pile of tires I asked you all to get cleaned up is still sitting there. Now, I understand we are all busy, but we must keep our house in order and that takes a team effort to do so. Let's please stay on top of these things. If you see an opportunity to make us look better, I need you to take it."

He continued.

"Also, there are many of you in this room who have been showing up late, leaving early, and not taking care of your CRM tasks efficiently. I don't need to name names because you know who you are but listen to me. If you're going to be away from your families for 12 hours a day, let's make sure you get a reward out of it. I am committed to doing everything in my power to make sure you are successful, but it has to be a two-way street. I need you to pull your weight, exceed what's expected of you, and don't take any shortcuts."

The team looked at him, and Alfred could tell something was immediately different. Instead of the looks of frustration, disappointment, or general disdain, they were far more engaged and seemingly empathetic to what he was saying. By starting off the meeting listening to them, and encouraging them, they were much more open to taking advice from him. It was a unique experience and felt amazing.

"On that note, we are going to make sure you have all of the tools and training necessary to extract everything you can out of this business. Being as sales is the lifeblood of what we do, one of the most important things you can learn is how to properly overcome objections. So, Gary and Vickey, please come up front."

Alfred then began working with the whole team on how to handle objections. This week he had decided to start with, "I have to think about it." So, he presented the objection and had Gary respond. Then he adjusted Gary's verbiage to help him understand exactly how to respond. He presented the same objection to Vickey. She responded, and he also adjusted hers. They went over it, and then went over it again, and then one more time for good measure. He did this with each member of the team, from the salespeople on the showroom floor, to the business development center reps that responded to leads, all the way up to his managers in each of their departments.

Of course, to top it all off, Alfred himself participated. They did this for about 20 minutes, and though it was a bit awkward at first, it got easier as things progressed. As the meeting wrapped up, Alfred had them all stand up. He had been saving a little something for the end of the meeting and was excited to share it. "Repeat after me please."

The team responded, and sentence by sentence Alfred shared a new mantra he had written that morning. He would say a sentence, then they would repeat it back, meanwhile he had the whole written mantra projected on the big screen.

"I am on a mission, to eradicate the negative stigmas associated with the car business. I can do this by making people feel special, feel important, and like they're the only one. I will offer an experience that exceeds my customers' expectations today, tomorrow, and in the future. I will not just sell cars; I will create fans!"

The team once again surged with clapping and cheering, and continued to do so as they made their way out of the meeting room.

Alfred sat back in awe and still couldn't believe it. He opened up his calendar and highlighted the day on it. Then he made a note inside, *Today is the day that everything changed.* He closed it back and let out a deep sigh of relief.

CHAPTER 8
A RARE MOMENT OF EXECUTION

> *"Great Things Are Not Done by Impulse,*
> *but by A Series of Small Things*
> *Brought Together."*
> **—Vincent van Gogh**

That night Alfred went home feeling accomplished and fulfilled. After heating up his dinner in the microwave, he sat down with a beer and his T.V. tray and began to eat quietly as the rest of the house was already asleep.

He put the game on the big screen, and then commenced to slowly eating while scrolling on his phone, with an occasional glance up at the screen to catch a touchdown pass, a punt return, or a running back breaking a tackle. While scrolling, he stumbled across a post from one of his favorite social media influencers, a guy by the name of Glenn Lundy, who had a long history of proven success in the auto industry, owned a company called 800% Elite Auto, and was also the host of a daily morning show that Alfred would listen to occasionally.

The post was about how long it truly takes to make or break a habit. Apparently, some study had been done by a prestigious college where they measured the actual biological changes in the human brain when picking up a new habit or dropping an old one.

The study showed that it takes sixty-seven days to create the new neural pathway that makes something easier to do, than to not do.

The example Glenn used was that if you want to become the type of person that works out, you need to work out every day for at least sixty-seven days straight. On day sixty-six it will be easier to NOT work out, on day sixty-seven it will be easier TO work out. It was fascinating.

Alfred thought about how the automotive world worked. Everything in his industry was set in thirty-day cycles. People got paid monthly. The manufacturers released rebates and incentives monthly. The goals were set monthly, the projections and targets were monthly, the bills, the financial statement, the performance metrics, literally everything was set in thirty-day windows.

Even when they would try a fresh marketing company, or some new software, or a new deal process, they always measured success in thirty-day windows, and were usually disappointed with the results.

There was even a known saying that Alfred and most everyone else used in the dealership on the first day of every single month: "Hero to zero." It didn't matter how well you did in the last month; it was a new month, and you were a zero in the new one.

Alfred began to think, "So if it takes sixty-seven days to make something easier to do, than to not do. Sixty-seven days to create a new habit or break an old one. How the heck can I expect anything to change around here in just thirty days?"

The question haunted him long into the night, and as the football game ended, and Alfred made his way to his bedroom, he decided at once that the daily morning meetings would happen every single day for at least the next sixty-seven days. Come hell or high water, he was going to make sure they happened.

The next morning Alfred followed the L.E.A.D.D. process again. He was the first one in the room, played upbeat instrumental music, started the meeting with positive Google reviews and employee highlights, and then he shared with them his concerns, and finished with some role-play around the same objection as the day before, "I have to think about it."

He ended the meeting with everyone reciting the mantra, "I am on a mission…" which he put on the projector again so that everyone could see and read it. Again, there was loud applause, and then the team went to work. It was great. A couple of people had walked in late, but other than that, he couldn't have asked for a better start to the day.

This behavior continued. Each day he held a meeting: Each day they followed the process, each day they chanted the mantra; each day they clapped and cheered. It was quite a stark contrast from how things used to happen, but more importantly, and quite surprisingly, sales started to pick up.

Deals were happening earlier in the day than they used to. Customers coming in, sales associates setting early appointments, breakfast runs down to a minimum, cold energy drinks…well those were STILL all the rage.

Alfred walked by a sales associate with her customer and heard the, "I need to think about it," objection being handled beautifully: "I understand you need to think about it," the sales associate said. "Most of my customers do. It's an especially important purchase, and to not be mindful of that would be irresponsible. So, let me ask you this, what is it about the deal that you need to think about most? Is it the payment? Or the down payment?"

The sales associate, with only 4 months of experience, was communicating with this customer in such a professional manner that it nearly brought a tear to Alfred's eye. "If only we had started this sooner," he thought.

The next few weeks were a blur. Alfred and the team had daily morning meetings, then the team went to work. They did all that they could throughout the day, and before Alfred knew it, September was over, and Smith Chevrolet had sold a record-breaking 162 cars for the month. Morale was over the top, and of course Alfred was more than pleased.

As the fall leaves began to change, the team at Smith Chevrolet continued to get dialed in and stack up some wins, and it felt like they were getting ready to have an amazing October.

Regretfully though, they were wrong.

As the month of October started to roll along, some unexpected challenges presented themselves. Seemingly out of nowhere, Alfred and the team ended up losing several key salespeople.

One guy named Joel decided to quit and retire early. Another named Keira quit because after 17 years in the business, she thought daily morning meetings were stupid, and a third salesperson, named

Willow, quit, and said it was because she was really tired from being on her feet all day, and she could tell things were changing around the dealership.

They all had a different reason for why they needed to leave, but the reality was that with all the recent changes, people were starting to be required to work outside of their comfort zones, and many of them didn't like it.

Even though in the beginning these salespeople participated and pretended to be into the meetings and the training, Alfred later found out that their enthusiasm was a façade. They only pretended to support the changes because they honestly didn't think it would last.

This was based on the fact that in the past it was pretty typical for Alfred to start new things, and then not be able to follow through with them. He would go to an event, come back excited, say things were going to change, and then thirty days later, either forget about the idea, or simply scrap it. It was quite humbling when he learned this truth, but he had to admit they weren't wrong.

At first Alfred was quite disappointed that they all had quit. Especially because for many years he had been taught to truly value employee retention. The loss of these long-time key players went against everything his dad and grandfather had taught him to stand for. But honestly, the more Alfred thought about it, the more he realized that holding on to people and allowing them to underperform really took a toll on the success of the business. Sure, retention is great, but could you imagine a professional sports team holding on to players just because they'd been on the team a long time? That doesn't make any sense.

In order to win championships, you have to have championship players, and that ultimately means there has to be seasons where people are growing, seasons where people are thriving, and seasons where people will burn out, and then of course there has to be seasons of change.

Though turbulent, October ended up a decent month. They were down a bit from the previous month, selling one hundred and twenty-nine cars, but it wasn't as bad as Alfred thought it was going to be considering how short staffed they were.

Then came November, and in November something magical happened, something that changed the trajectory of Smith Chevrolet forever.

It had been sixty-seven days since Smith Chevrolet had started daily morning meetings. Sixty-seven days of Listening, Encouraging, Advising, and Developing, Daily. Sixty-seven days of making the people who showed up late to the morning meetings buy breakfast for those that were on time. (In a fun way and encouraging way.) Sixty-seven days of celebrating the behaviors Alfred wanted to see more of. Sixty-seven days of repeating the mantra, over and over no matter how many people were rolling their eyes during the process. Sixty-seven days of role-playing and objection handling. Sixty-seven days…nearly two and a half months, and suddenly, something clicked.

Alfred could've sworn he heard it audibly. "Did you hear that?" he asked Doreen, who was in his office going over marketing reports.

"Hear what?" Doreen responded.

Alfred got up and walked out of his office and towards the main area. As he approached, he could hear the slight murmur of a busy showroom. He looked left and saw a set of customers working with his top salesman. He looked right and he could see his new Sales Manager working with three salespeople. The radio was on K-Love playing upbeat Christian music. Other salespeople were typing on their computers, and sending text messages, and he saw one salesperson recording a video.

He looked at the sales board, and though it was only 10:30 A.M. they had already sold three cars for the day. The entire place was visibly, and audibly different, and the energy was electric.

Somehow being short-staffed had invigorated the remaining team members. At the same time, the loss of key salespeople on the floor had solidified the production of the ones that were still there. The daily training was working, and team members across the board were acting and performing with a completely different level of professionalism.

EVERYTHING was different, from the daily activities to the results, and even the "sounds" of the dealership. Things were so different that Alfred had actually heard the shift, and as November ended, Smith Chevrolet broke an all-time record, putting one hundred sixty-seven vehicles in the driveways of families all around the area.

Alfred went back to his office and into his bathroom. He looked in the mirror intently and smiled at the reflection smiling back. Even he looked different. He barely recognized the guy in the mirror. His morning routine had helped him lose twelve pounds. The bags under his eyes had faded away. His confidence and bravado were shining through. He actually liked the man he saw in the mirror.

He sat there in a moment of proud reflection, and for an instant thought he noticed a figure outside of his own in the mirror. He couldn't quite get it in focus, but in a weird way, he could've sworn it looked very much like his grandfather.

Special Offer

Elevate Your Mornings.
Transform Your Life

Inspired by Alfred's journey and the transformative power of the Morning 5? Are you ready to revolutionize the way you start your day, both personally and in your business? We have an exclusive offer just for our valued readers!

Unlock Your Free 'Morning 5' Planner and E-book!

As a reader of "The Legacy Titles - A Parable for Success - 12 Proven Principles to Grow Your Business 800%", you have a unique opportunity to dive deeper into the Morning 5 philosophy. With this special offer, you'll receive:

1. **A Free Morning 5 Planner PDF:** This comprehensive planner is designed to help you implement the Morning 5 routine effectively, ensuring you start each day with purpose, clarity, and on a path towards success.

2. **A Free Copy of The Morning 5 E-book by Glenn Lundy:** Delve into the e-book that started it all. Written by Glenn Lundy, this insightful guide expands on the principles introduced in the Morning 5 Title, offering practical advice and inspiring stories to kickstart your transformative morning journey.

How to Claim Your Free Gifts:

It's simple! Just scan the QR code below with your smartphone. You'll be taken directly to a page where you can download both the Morning 5 Planner and The Morning 5 E-book instantly.

Don't miss this chance to reshape your mornings and set a new tone for your life and business. Like Alfred, you can harness the power of starting your day with intention and focus. Scan the code, grab your free resources, and embark on a journey of personal and professional transformation with the Morning 5!

CHAPTER 9
WHAT DO YOU WANT?

Title II

- CERTIFICATE OF TITLE NUMBER II -

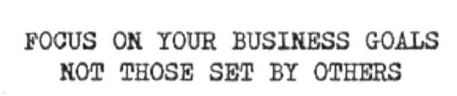

FOCUS ON YOUR BUSINESS GOALS
NOT THOSE SET BY OTHERS

UNDERSTAND AND ABSORB DEEPLY INTO YOUR VERY ESSENCE, DILIGENT MERCHANT, THE TEACHINGS OF THIS TITLE MARKED II, FOR WITHIN ITS FABRIC LIES A TRUTH AS ANCIENT AND UNYIELDING AS THE MOUNTAINS. "FOCUS ON YOUR BUSINESS GOALS, NOT THOSE SET BY OTHERS," IT PROCLAIMS WITH A VOICE STEADY AND UNWAVERING.

IN THE BUSTLING MARKETPLACE OF COMMERCE, A SYMPHONY OF VOICES RISE, EACH OFFERING ADVICE, SUGGESTING PATHS, AND IMPOSING VISIONS. AMIDST THIS CHORUS, YOU MAY FIND YOURSELF ADRIFT, PULLED IN VARIOUS DIRECTIONS BY THE WHIMS AND OBJECTIVES OF OTHERS, EACH WITH A VISION OF SUCCESS DIFFERING FROM YOUR OWN UNIQUE PERSPECTIVE.

UNDER THE EXPANSIVE SKY, ON THIS STAGE OF ENDEAVOR AND UNRELENTING PURSUIT, YOU MUST WEAR YOUR VISION AS A CROWN, ALLOWING IT TO ILLUMINATE YOUR PATH WITH A RADIANCE SO RESPLENDENT AND DISTINCTIVE THAT IT CANNOT BE DIMMED OR ALTERED BY THE MULTITUDE OF OTHER LIGHTS FLICKERING AT THE PERIPHERY.

YOUR GOALS, TIRELESS ONE, MUST BE FORGED IN THE CRUCIBLE OF YOUR OWN UNDERSTANDING AND DESIRE, SHAPED BY HANDS THAT HAVE FELT THE HEARTBEAT OF YOUR DREAMS AND THE RHYTHM OF YOUR DEEPEST ASPIRATIONS. FOR IF YOU EMBARK UPON THE TUMULTUOUS SEAS OF ENTERPRISE WITH A COMPASS CALIBRATED BY ANOTHER, YOU MAY FIND YOUR VESSEL TOSSED AND TURNED, VEERING AWAY FROM THE HARBORS YOU SEEK TO REACH.

DO NOT LET THE SHADOWS OF ANOTHER'S DREAM OBSCURE THE VISTAS OF YOUR OWN IMAGINATION. OTHERS MAY ENVISION MOUNTAINS OF GOLD, EXPANSES GLEAMING WITH THE ALLURE OF UNTOLD WEALTH, YET IF YOUR SOUL IS DRAWN TO THE TRANQUIL VALLEYS OF CONTENTMENT AND STEADY PROGRESS, THEN DO NOT LET THE DAZZLE OF THEIR VISION BLIND YOU.

STAND FIRM AND UNWAVERING, LIKE THE MIGHTY OAK AMIDST THE FOREST, IT'S ROOTS DEEPLY EMBEDDED IN THE SOIL, DRAWING NOURISHMENT FROM THE SPRINGS OF SELF-AWARENESS AND CLARITY. WHEN THE WINDS HOWL AND VOICES, WHETHER DRAPED IN THE GUISE OF WELL-WISHERS OR SEASONED ADVISORS, TEMPT YOU TO CHANGE COURSE, TO ADOPT AMBITIONS NOT OF YOUR OWN MAKING, LET THE ECHOES OF TITLE MARKED II RESOUND CLEARLY AND RESOLUTELY IN YOUR EARS.

"FOCUS ON YOUR BUSINESS GOALS," IT GENTLY REMINDS, YET WITH AN AUTHORITY ROOTED IN TIMELESS WISDOM, "NOT THOSE SET BY OTHERS."

IN THIS NEVER-ENDING THEATER OF STRIVING, LET YOUR GOALS BE THE STARS THAT GUIDE YOU, THE LIGHTHOUSES THAT STEER YOU AWAY FROM TREACHEROUS SHOALS. WITH YOUR GAZE FIXED STEADFASTLY ON THESE BEACONS, NAVIGATE WITH CONFIDENCE AND DETERMINATION, FOR THE SHORES YOU APPROACH BEAR THE PROMISE OF A SUCCESS TRULY YOUR OWN, A TRIUMPH THAT ECHOES THE MELODIES OF YOUR OWN SONG-SWEET, HARMONIOUS, AND UNQUESTIONABLY, UNIQUELY YOURS.

> *"Your Time is Limited, Don't Waste it*
> *Living Someone Else's Life."*
> —Steve Jobs

Alfred decided now that he and the team had been practicing "The Morning 5" routine and following the L.E.A.D.D. process for some time, they were ready to start focusing on the next Title in the chest. He made his way to his office, collected the chest from his office safe, and began to read:

The Title Marked II

Focus on Your Business Goals, not those Set by Others

Understand and absorb deeply into your very essence, diligent merchant, the teachings of this Title Marked II, for within its fabric lies a truth as ancient and unyielding as the mountains. "Focus on YOUR Business Goals, not Those Set by Others," it proclaims with a voice steady and unwavering.

In the bustling marketplace of commerce, a symphony of voices rise, each offering advice, suggesting paths, and imposing visions. Amidst this chorus, you may find yourself adrift, pulled in various directions by the whims and objectives of others, each with a vision of success differing from your own unique perspective.

Under the expansive sky, on this stage of endeavor and unrelenting pursuit, you must wear your vision as a crown, allowing it to illuminate your path with a radiance so resplendent and distinctive that it cannot be dimmed or altered by the multitude of other lights flickering at the periphery.

Your goals, tireless one, must be forged in the crucible of your own understanding and desire, shaped by hands that have felt the heartbeat of your dreams and the rhythm of your deepest aspirations. For if you embark upon the tumultuous seas of enterprise with a compass calibrated by another, you may find your vessel tossed and turned, veering away from the harbors you seek to reach.

Do not let the shadows of another's dream obscure the vistas of your own imagination. Others may envision mountains of gold, expanses gleaming with the allure of untold wealth, yet if your soul is drawn to the tranquil valleys of contentment and steady progress, then do not let the dazzle of their vision blind you.

Stand firm and unwavering, like the mighty oak amidst the forest, its roots deeply embedded in the soil, drawing nourishment from the springs of self-awareness and clarity. When the winds howl and voices, whether draped in the guise of well-wishers or seasoned advisors, tempt you to change course, to adopt ambitions not of your own making, let the echoes of Title Marked II resound clearly and resolutely in your ears.

"Focus on YOUR Business Goals," it gently reminds, yet with authority rooted in timeless wisdom, "not those Set by Others."

In this never-ending theater of striving, let your goals be the stars that guide you, the lighthouses that steer you away from treacherous shores. With your gaze fixed steadfastly on these beacons, navigate with confidence and determination, for the shorelines you approach bear the promise of a success truly your own, a triumph that echoes the melodies of your own song—sweet, harmonious, and unquestionably, uniquely yours.

Unlike "The Morning 5" Title, the Title Marked II gave Alfred a sense of relief. He had been truly tired of living his life by other people's standards. For as long as he could remember, he had always felt the weight of his family name and, even heavier, his grandfather's legacy. The idea of being able to carve his own path appealed to him.

As his mind processed it again, he really began to see how utterly different this Title was from his current mental process. Every goal he had ever set in the store (and most likely in his life), was influenced in one way or another by someone on the outside.

Chevrolet sent him their goals every month, every quarter, and even came into his dealership once a year to forecast the next twelve months.

Alfred's twenty group, where he went four times a year to meet up with nineteen other dealers roughly the same size in sales volume as him, spent most of their time together projecting, forecasting, and setting goals based on market trends, previous performance, and the agreed upon industry standards (when they weren't drinking beers of course). None of this was open to individual interpretation.

Even at home, Alfred was setting and hitting goals that didn't matter in the grander scheme of things. Sure, they had a nice house, a small yard, and the proverbial white picket fence, but none of those things were really his goals. He had simply done an excellent job of keeping up with the Joneses. His grass looked amazing, and his house was a decent size compared to the neighbors in the neighborhood, but outside that, there was really no substance. The more Alfred thought about it, the more he realized he was living someone else's idea of what his life should look like.

With Title in hand, Alfred decided he was going to change all of that. He was going to focus on his unique goals and throw out anyone else's idea of what is possible for him. He was fed up with people telling him what he should be doing, and it was time for Alfred to trust himself.

The next day Alfred sat in his office and contemplated what he thought the dealership should be able to accomplish in the next month. "180 cars? 200? Is that a reasonable target?" he asked himself. "Is my team going to think I'm just pulling a number out of thin air? Are they going to trust me moving forward if I do set a target and we don't hit it? Shouldn't I just be happy with where we are?" He continued to think through things "How have I always done it in the past, and how can it be done differently this time?"

The last thought struck a chord. "How I have always done it…" Alfred began to take notes. As he thought back, he realized as a company they always had a monthly goal, but never anything beyond that. Yearly goals, five-year goals, ten-year goals. None of that ever factored in. It was simply a matter of how many cars they could sell in a month. The entire business operated thirty days at a time.

"No wonder we can never change anything around here. It takes sixty-seven days before something becomes easier to do than to not do, and yet we are only focused on what we can accomplish in 30-day windows." Alfred thought again. He was a bit taken aback by what had now become a purely natural thought. Clearly, the Titles, which he had been reading repeatedly, were working on more than just the business. They were working on him.

The decision was made to do things differently this time. Instead of just setting a monthly goal, and hoping for the best, he was going to take some time and map out a yearly goal, broken down into quarters, further broken down into months, and ultimately broken down into days. This would allow him to use actual data from the previous year, and to be able to note trends and adjust for any possible market shifts, like holiday season, summer season, tax season, etc.

He started with the first month coming up, December, and began to take notes:

25 business days in the month.

Closed for Christmas day.

The last week of the month is always the busiest of the year.

Last year sold 115 cars.

Alfred then decided he would look at how many cars were sold on each individual day last year:

Friday Dec. 1st – 3 cars

Saturday Dec. 2nd – 5 cars.

Monday Dec. 4th – 3 cars

Tuesday Dec. 5th – 2 cars

Wednesday Dec. 6th – 2 cars

Thursday Dec. 7th – 3 cars

Friday Dec. 8th – 4 cars

Saturday Dec. 9th – 3 cars.

He continued for the rest of December. Once he had all the totals, he looked at them carefully and thought about what the next step should be.

After careful consideration, he decided he would fill in this year's calendar based on each of last year's daily sold numbers, and then set a goal to increase 25% over last year. NOT 25% OVER LAST MONTH, like he normally would do, but over LAST YEAR. December to December. It was important for him to compare apples to apples, and oranges to oranges, and history had shown that each month of the year had its own intricacies that came along with it. Things like weather conditions, school starting or finishing for the year, winter vs. spring, etc.

He then began going day by day, looking at last year, and then calculating what the goal would be with a 25% increase. As he began to do so, he quickly identified that the actual dates didn't match one year to the next. Friday this year was the 3rd. Last year Friday was the 1st. So instead of comparing the actual dates of December (Like comparing the 5th of last year's December to the 5th of December this year), he would instead compare the days of the week. The first Monday of last December would be compared with the first Monday of this December. The third Thursday from last year, would be compared to the 3rd Thursday of this year, and so on.

Now, the date would be different, but the actual day of the week would be the same.

Alfred was now able to have a daily goal, which would feed the monthly goal, that ultimately fed the yearly goal, and it was all based on actual data specific to Smith Chevrolet.

When complete, Alfred diligently placed the daily goals one-by-one on the calendar with a green marker. It was Christmas season after all. As soon as he did that it triggered something in him. Red always reminded Alfred of something bad. If your bank account was in the red, bad news. A red "X" on a test meant that question was wrong. Stop signs…Red.

Green on the other hand was a wonderful thing. Green is the color of money. Green check marks on his paper meant he got the answer right. A green light…Go.

As Alfred was thinking through this, he got a got a text from his wife, Betty. She had been working on potty training their son Fischer, and to her delight he had gone pee-pee in the potty. She asked if Alfred had a minute to celebrate.

Alfred dialed her immediately and, in an instant, he could hear Fischer on the other end of the line. "Fischer went pee-pee in the potty, Fischer went pee-pee in the potty! Fischer went pee-pee in the potty! Cause he's a really big boy!" Alfred sang with delight. He could hear Fischer's smile as he responded to the encouragement from his dad.

They got off the phone and Alfred sat back in thought, "Here we go again!"

He was referring to Lucy's potty-training experience, and also the way they had implemented celebrations into the morning meetings. He quickly jotted down a note. *"Green is good, and people love to be celebrated."* He now knew exactly what he needed to do.

Racing to the nearest Office Max, Alfred went in and grabbed a big whiteboard calendar. It wasn't numbered but had a little space to write in the numbers for each day. He took it back to his office and started copying the numbers for December he had put on his calendar onto the new whiteboard. Once he was done, the whiteboard looked like this.

DECEMBER						
Sun	Mon	Tue	Wed	Thu	Fri	Sat
1 /	2 / 4	3 / 3	4 / 3	5 / 4	6 / 5	7 / 4
8 /	9 / 3	10 / 5	11 / 2	12 / 4	13 / 3	14 / 6
15 /	16 / 2	17 / 4	18 / 5	19 / 3	20 / 2	21 / 5
22 /	23 / 5	24 / 3	25 /	26 / 4	27 / 5	28 / 3
29 /	30 / 7	31 / 5	1 /	2 /	3 /	4 /

NOTES:

Alfred then headed out to the sales floor and hung the whiteboard directly in the sales tower. He positioned it so that it was in plain in sight of every manager, every salesperson, and potentially any customer that walked by. He wanted everyone to know what the goal was for the day, and what it took to be "Green" and what it took to be celebrated.

It wasn't long before his team started asking him questions about the newest addition to their showroom décor.

"What the heck is this all about?" they inquired.

Alfred broke it down for them very simply. "The numbers you see on the board are based on last year's data. The Fridays from this year are matched up with the Fridays from last year. The Tuesdays match the Tuesdays, Saturdays match the Saturdays, etc. The game is simple. Sell enough cars to match or exceed the number on that board, and we will celebrate. Come up short, and we won't. Simple as that."

Over the next few days, after the morning meetings, Alfred made sure everyone paid attention to the daily goal. He would ask around making sure people knew what the target was and would celebrate like crazy if they matched or exceeded the number.

On any given night he could be found jumping around, waving his arms, dancing around with delight, singing their praises, and acting just like he would every time Fischer went pee-pee in the potty.

The response from his team was palpable and immediate. They would come in each day and check the board. In the evenings they would do everything in their power to hit those green days and would join in on the celebrations. Anytime they didn't hit the number Alfred would write how many they sold on the board in red. On those days he wouldn't say a word. He didn't discipline them, he didn't reprimand them, nothing. Just silence. A silence that had a far more profound impact than any words ever could.

By the end of December, Alfred and his team had put up twenty-one green days, and only five red days, leading the team to break an all-time December sales record and grow a whopping 27% year-over-year.

The board had allowed Alfred to do exactly what the Title Marked II had prescribed. He had set his own goals one day at a time, and in exchange had driven massive results that far exceeded anything General Motors, or his twenty group, would've ever predicted. It had only been four months since Alfred's grandfather had passed away and left him the Titles, and he was already selling nearly 40% more cars than ever before.

Alfred was even more impressed by how simple most of it was. It took work, intentionality, discipline, and accountability, but in retrospect they were not reinventing the wheel here. Just making a few little tweaks, which were going a long, long way.

CHAPTER 10
THERE ARE DIAMONDS RIGHT BENEATH YOUR FEET

Title III

- CERTIFICATE OF TITLE NUMBER III -

PROMOTE FROM WITHIN

AS THE DAWN HERALDS A NEW DAY, UNFOLDING BEFORE MY EYES LIKE A BLANK CANVAS, READY TO BE ADORNED WITH BOTH SMALL AND GREAT DEEDS, I INSCRIBE UPON IT A PRINCIPLE OF UTMOST SIGNIFICANCE: "PROMOTE FROM WITHIN."

WITHIN THE VERY WALLS THAT SHELTER MY ENTERPRISE, AMONG THE MEN AND WOMEN WHO LABOR UNDER ITS BANNER, LIES A RESERVOIR OF UNTAPPED TALENT, AN UNEXPLORED WELL OF POTENTIAL. THESE INDIVIDUALS, WHOSE HANDS ARE SHAPED AND STRENGTHENED BY THE DAILY WORK THEY PERFORM, POSSESS A WISDOM THAT IS BOTH UNIQUE AND INVALUABLE.

AS THE SUN RISES, CASTING ITS RADIANT LIGHT UPON THE EARTH, ILLUMINATING HIDDEN CORNERS AND SHADOWED VALLEYS, SO SHALL I STRIVE TO SHED LIGHT ON THE LATENT GIFTS AND ABILITIES RESIDING WITHIN MY TEAM. WITH EYES FREE FROM PREJUDICE AND HEARTS UNBURDENED BY FAVORITISM, I SHALL OBSERVE, EVALUATE, AND RECOGNIZE THE QUIET CONTRIBUTIONS AND UNSEEN SACRIFICES.

FOR WITHIN EACH PERSON WHO WALKS BESIDE ME IN THE PURSUIT OF OUR COLLECTIVE DREAMS AND GOALS, THERE LIES A LEADER WAITING TO BE AWAKENED, A COMMANDER EAGER TO BE CALLED INTO SERVICE. IT IS NOT JUST MY DUTY, BUT MY PRIVILEGE, TO NURTURE AND CULTIVATE LEADERSHIP POTENTIAL UNTIL IT BURSTS FORTH IN A BLAZE OF GLORY AND BRILLIANCE.

TO PROMOTE FROM WITHIN IS NOT MERELY A STRATEGIC CHOICE: IT IS A PACT, A PROMISE WOVEN FROM THE THREADS OF TRUST AND BELIEF. IT IS THE SILENT ASSURANCE THAT SAYS, "I SEE YOU. I ACKNOWLEDGE YOUR WORTH AND VALUE. YOUR EFFORTS HAVE NOT GONE UNNOTICED." IT IS THE RALLYING CRY THAT STIRS DORMANT ASPIRATIONS, IGNITING A SPARK OF HOPE AND AMBITION.

AS THE DAY UNFOLDS, WITNESSING THE CEASELESS DANCE OF TIME AND TIDE, I AM COMMITTED TO FOSTERING AN ENVIRONMENT WHERE GROWTH IS NOT JUST ENCOURAGED BUT CELEBRATED. WHERE THE SEEDS OF POTENTIAL, ONCE SOWN, ARE NOURISHED WITH OPPORTUNITY, BATHED IN THE SUNLIGHT OF ENCOURAGEMENT, AND SHIELDED FROM THE FROST OF DISCOURAGEMENT.

IN THE SACRED SCRIPT OF LEADERSHIP, "PROMOTE FROM WITHIN" SHALL BE THE VERSE I RECITE IN MOMENTS OF DECISION, THE MANTRA THAT GUIDES MY HAND AS I NAVIGATE THE WATERS OF RESPONSIBILITY AND EXPECTATION. IT SHALL BE THE NORTH STAR THAT GUIDES ME THROUGH THE DARKEST OF NIGHTS, LEADING ME TOWARD THE DAWN OF SUCCESS AND FULFILLMENT.

AS TWILIGHT CASTS LONG SHADOWS ACROSS THE LAND, AND I CLOSE MY EYES IN PREPARATION FOR THE MORROW, MY HEART SHALL BE LIGHT, BUOYED BY THE KNOWLEDGE THAT WITHIN MY REALM, TALENT HAS FOUND ITS RIGHTFUL PLACE, POTENTIAL HAS BEEN RECOGNIZED, AND LEADERSHIP HAS BEEN NURTURED AND PROMOTED FROM WITHIN.

WITH THE TITLE MARKED III HELD FIRMLY IN MY HANDS, I STEP FORWARD INTO THE NEW DAY, MY GAZE FIXED UPON THE HORIZON OF POSSIBILITY. I AM READY TO UNEARTH AND ELEVATE THE HIDDEN GEMS WITHIN MY TEAM, PROMOTING FROM WITHIN, AND BUILDING A LEGACY OF EMPOWERMENT AND TRUST. IN THE TAPESTRY OF SUCCESS, EVERY THREAD IS VITAL, AND EVERY STRAND, NO MATTER HOW INCONSPICUOUS, CONTRIBUTES TO THE MASTERPIECE OF ACHIEVEMENT.

"Do nothing out of selfish ambition or vain conceit. Rather, in humility, value others above yourselves, not looking to your own interests but each of you to the interests of the others."
—Philippians 2:3-4 (NIV)

The daily goal board, mixed with daily meetings, mixed with consistent celebrations, mixed with training, mixed with role-playing, mixed with Alfred doing his Morning 5, mixed with everyone of Alfred's leaders understanding the L.E.A.D.D. process, had in just a matter of four months completely transformed the culture at Smith Chevrolet.

They were now starting every day with intention and purpose, and everyone on the team understood the flow of things. Alfred felt it was time to tap into the next Title. He pulled down the wooden chest, opened it up, and rifled through the Titles excited to see what was next:

The Title Marked III
Promote from Within

As the dawn heralds a new day, unfolding before my eyes like a blank canvas, ready to be adorned with both small and great deeds, I inscribe upon it a principle of utmost significance: "Promote from Within."

Within the very walls that shelter my enterprise, among the men and women who labor under its banner, lies a reservoir of untapped talent, an unexplored well of potential. These individuals, whose hands are shaped and strengthened by the daily work they perform, possess a wisdom that is both unique and invaluable.

As the sun rises, casting its radiant light upon the earth, illuminating hidden corners and shadowed valleys, so shall I strive to shed light on the latent gifts and abilities residing within my team. With eyes free from prejudice and hearts unburdened by favoritism, I shall observe, evaluate, and recognize the quiet contributions and unseen sacrifices.

For within each person who walks beside me in the pursuit of our collective dreams and goals, there lies a leader waiting to be awakened, a commander eager to be called into service. It is not just my duty, but my privilege, to nurture and cultivate leadership potential until it bursts forth in a blaze of glory and brilliance.

To promote from within is not merely a strategic choice; it is a pact, a promise woven from the threads of trust and belief. It is the silent assurance that says, "I see you. I acknowledge your worth and value. Your efforts have not gone unnoticed." It is the rallying cry that stirs dormant aspirations, igniting a spark of hope and ambition.

As the day unfolds, witnessing the ceaseless dance of time and tide, I am committed to fostering an environment where growth is not just encouraged but celebrated. Where the seeds of potential, once sown, are nourished with opportunity, bathed in the sunlight of encouragement, and shielded from the frost of discouragement.

In the sacred script of leadership, "Promote from Within" shall be the verse I recite in moments of decision, the mantra that guides my hand as I navigate the waters of responsibility and expectation. It shall be the North Star that guides me through the darkest of nights, leading me toward the dawn of success and fulfillment.

As twilight casts long shadows across the land, and I close my eyes in preparation for the morrow, my heart shall be light, buoyed by the knowledge that within my realm, talent has found its rightful place, potential has been recognized, and leadership has been nurtured and promoted from within.

With the Title Marked III held firmly in my hands, I step forward into the new day, my gaze fixed upon the horizon of possibility. I am ready to unearth and elevate the hidden gems within my team, promoting from within, and building a legacy of empowerment and trust. In the tapestry of success, every thread is vital, and every strand, no matter how inconspicuous, contributes to the masterpiece of achievement.

Alfred tried to think back to the last promotion he'd given in the store...he couldn't remember. It had been so long. Most of his managers had been in place for years, and since the dealership had not been growing, there was no reason to add anyone.

Even those that he did have in place were hired from outside the organization. His finance manager was recruited from a store on the other side of town, his controller from another state, and both his sales managers came from other stores as well. This one was going to be something Alfred would really need time to wrap his mind around.

He continued contemplating, the words now inscribed in his mind in a manner that would certainly last forever. Up until this point, his team had done a fantastic job managing the increase in sales, but he could tell they were running a little bit thin. His sales managers were constantly working deals, his finance department was getting behind at times, and there were multiple salespeople that were looking for advancement in their careers. There was one problem though, a promotion from within would thin out the sales floor, and if Alfred were honest, they had not done a decent job training people for a new role.

Then Alfred remembered that at one of his twenty group meetings, a fellow dealer had mentioned something he called "The Triplets." Apparently, this dealer had selected three of their salespeople that they felt had potential to be leaders in the organization one day. They sat down with each of one of them and explained the opportunity they had in front of them.

After it was clear they understood the opportunity, the dealer then laid out a series of job duties, and expectations, which would prepare them for the next level. He told them he would pay them a little extra for the additional workload, but they were still required to maintain the highest level when it came to their sales.

So, Alfred pulled out a sheet of paper and broke down what it took to be a great salesperson AND he also noted the requirements of someone in a leadership position:

Maintains at least 20 deals a month.

Has above average customer satisfaction scores.

Shows up to meetings on time and enthusiastic.

Is willing to support and train new salespeople.

Understands how to read credit bureaus and submit to banks for loan approvals.

Can appraise a used vehicle.

Knows how to handle objections.

Maintains their composure in heated situations.

Communicates well and gets along with others.

Good at basic math.

Reliable, trustworthy, and energetic.

Relentless work ethic.

Strong closer.

Organized and efficient at filling out the appropriate paperwork.

Has a burning desire to succeed.

Alfred sat back and looked at the list. There were three names that immediately came to mind as he looked through it: Jessica, Brandon, and Nick. These three could be his "Triplets."

The success of the previous Titles had given Alfred a newfound confidence when it came to making decisions, so he immediately called all three of them to his office.

When they arrived, he explained to them that from this point forward Smith Chevrolet would always be a company that would promote from within. A new role would be created to educate them on what the next level looked like, while also requiring them to maintain their current positions. It would be a challenging role, but would have a small salary attached to it, and if they were successful in the new role, it would ultimately lead to a promotion.

He then went through the list of job requirements he had written down earlier, and asked if they would be interested in the position. All three came back with a resounding "Yes!"

Alfred then pulled in his current management staff and informed them of his decision. They were to train Jessica, Brandon, and Nick in all the caveats of their positions, while also holding them accountable to their current results. Doreen specifically seemed elated, and relieved. Apparently, the increase in sales had put a little more pressure on her than Alfred had anticipated, but of course, being the type of person she was, she had never once complained. They all agreed, and just like that, the Triplets were born.

The next morning Alfred used the morning meeting to announce to the rest of the team his decision. He brought the newly formed "Triplets" to the front of the room and explained how they would now be an additional resource for everyone in the dealership. They could help close deals, appraise cars, answer any questions, etc.

It was made clear that they were still salespeople with the same responsibilities of that role, but that others could also now benefit from the Triplets wisdom and experience. Alfred also made sure to let everyone know that going forward the company would be promoting from within as they grew, and that more "Triplet" positions would open in the future as members of the newly formed threesome were promoted, or if necessary, demoted.

Alfred also used this moment to remind the team that growth was required for new positions to open up. If they continue to sell the same number of cars, the only time promotions could occur was if someone were to quit, or get fired, which happened rarely in management positions. However, if they kept increasing sales, naturally, more positions would be created.

Everyone understood, and the Smith Chevrolet Triplets began their new roles.

The next day the energy in the dealership was electric. The Triplets were running around doing everything they normally did, but also jumping in and helping others. At times Alfred would see one of them sitting next to a finance manager learning how to contract a deal, and at other times he would see one of them jump right in and close a deal for a newer salesperson. It was amazing because though they still hadn't solved the issue of being short-staffed, it seemed with the extra energy, everyone was able to do more.

Somehow, magically it seemed, the workload seemed lighter, and efficiencies increased. It had only been a day, but Alfred knew this was going to change the trajectory of Smith Chevrolet for decades to come.

He couldn't help but think that for over fifty years they had always gone outside to hire leaders and would only hire them when they had to. It was always a situation where someone quit, or someone got fired, and now the company's back was against the wall. With this new process they would now be proactive in filling future roles instead of reactive. It was simple actually; Alfred couldn't believe he hadn't thought of it before.

"But hey, the best time to plant a tree was ten years ago, the second-best time is now." Alfred could hear the voice of Les Brown echo in his mind. So much truth to this powerful little sentence.

CHAPTER 11
FAIL TO PLAN AND YOU PLAN TO FAIL

Title IV

- CERTIFICATE OF TITLE NUMBER IV -

THE 8-5-3-1 FORMULA

AS THE GOLDEN TAPESTRY OF DAWN UNFOLDS ACROSS THE SKY, I UNFURL THE TITLE MARKED IV, ALLOWING ITS WISDOM TO ILLUMINATE MY PATH WITH THE BRILLIANCE OF THE 8-5-3-1 FORMULA-A SACRED SEQUENCE THAT WHISPERS THE SECRET RHYTHMS OF SUCCESS.

WITH THE FIRST LIGHT OF DAWN, MY JOURNEY BEGINS. EIGHT LEADS, AKIN TO THE CARDINAL POINTS ON AN ANCIENT COMPASS, SHALL SERVE AS MY GUIDES THROUGH THE VAST SEAS OF OPPORTUNITY. THESE ARE NOT MERE NAMES OR NUMBERS BUT LIVING, BREATHING ENTITIES WITH DESIRES, HOPES, AND NEEDS SIMILAR TO MY OWN. I SHALL APPROACH EACH LEAD NOT AS A CONQUEROR BUT AS A SERVANT, OFFERING ASSISTANCE RATHER THAN INSISTENCE, AND PROVIDING VALUE THAT RESONATES WITH THE SYMPHONY OF THEIR ASPIRATIONS.

OUT OF THE ABUNDANT EIGHT, I SHALL CAREFULLY CULTIVATE A GARDEN OF FIVE APPOINTMENTS. THESE APPOINTMENTS ARE THE BRIDGES THAT CONNECT THE ISLANDS OF OPPORTUNITY, AND IT IS MY DUTY TO ENSURE THAT THESE BRIDGES ARE STURDY, WELCOMING, AND ACTIVELY USED. EACH APPOINTMENT IS A DANCE, A DELICATE BALLET OF GIVING AND RECEIVING, UNDERSTANDING AND EXPLAINING, LISTENING AND SPEAKING. WITH OPEN EARS AND AN OPEN HEART, I SHALL ENTER THESE APPOINTMENTS, SOWING THE SEEDS OF TRUST AND NURTURING THEM WITH RELIABILITY AND RESPECT.

YET, THE TITLE SAGELY REMINDS ME, NOT ALL SEEDS SHALL SPROUT, NOT ALL FLOWERS SHALL BLOOM. OF THE FIVE APPOINTMENTS NURTURED WITH CARE AND COMMITMENT, THREE SHALL BEAR FRUIT. THESE THREE APPOINTMENTS THAT MATERIALIZE INTO REALITY ARE PRECIOUS, AND I SHALL TREAT THEM AS SUCH-WITH RESPECT, FOCUS, AND UNPARALLELED SERVICE. WITHIN THE REALM OF THESE APPOINTMENTS, I SHALL NOT MERELY BE A SALESPERSON BUT A GUIDE, AN ADVISOR, A CONSULTANT WHOSE PRIMARY AIM IS TO ILLUMINATE THE PATH FOR THE CLIENT, MAKING THEIR JOURNEY ENJOYABLE, STRAIGHTFORWARD, AND REWARDING.

IN THE GRAND TAPESTRY OF THE DAY, AMIDST THE DANCE OF APPOINTMENTS AND THE MELODY OF LEADS, ONE CAR SHALL FIND ITS NEW OWNER. THIS IS NOT JUST A TRANSACTION BUT A TRANSFORMATION-A MOMENT WHERE DREAMS ARE HANDED KEYS, ASPIRATIONS SETTLE INTO THE DRIVER'S SEAT, AND POSSIBILITIES ARE IGNITED WITH THE TURN OF AN ENGINE. SELLING ONE CAR REPRESENTS MORE THAN A FINANCIAL GAIN: IT SIGNIFIES THE BLOSSOMING OF RELATIONSHIPS, THE ESTABLISHMENT OF TRUST, AND THE BUILDING OF OUR DEALERSHIP'S LEGACY AS A BEACON OF SERVICE AND VALUE.

THE 8-5-3-1 FORMULA IS NOT RIGID, BUT FLUID, ADAPTABLE TO THE EBBS AND FLOWS OF THE MARKETPLACE, RESPONSIVE TO THE UNIQUE NUANCES OF EACH CLIENT. EACH NUMBER IN THIS SACRED SEQUENCE SERVES AS A STEPPINGSTONE, GUIDING ME ACROSS THE RIVER OF THE DAY TOWARD THE SHORES OF SUCCESS, WHERE THE FRUIT OF ONE CAR SOLD AWAITS, RIPE AND READY FOR HARVEST.

WITH THE TITLE MARKED IV CLUTCHED CLOSE TO MY HEART, BEARING THE SACRED 8-5-3-1 FORMULA INSCRIBED UPON IT, I STEP FORWARD INTO THE DAY. MY EYES ARE ALIGHT WITH PURPOSE, MY HEART IS BRIMMING WITH A COMMITMENT TO SERVICE. FOR WITHIN THE NUMERICAL DANCE OF EIGHT LEADS, FIVE APPOINTMENTS SET, THREE APPOINTMENTS KEPT, AND ONE CAR SOLD, LIES THE SYMPHONY OF SUCCESS-A MELODY OF PROSPERITY AND FULFILLMENT, NOT ONLY FOR MYSELF BUT FOR ALL WHO ENTER OUR HALLOWED DEALERSHIP DOORS.

WITH THE TITLE IN HAND, I ADVANCE, READY TO EMBODY AND ENACT THE SACRED RHYTHM, THE HEARTBEAT OF SUCCESS: THE 8-5-3-1 FORMULA. FOR WITHIN ITS SIMPLICITY LIES UNMATCHED POWER, WITHIN ITS NUMBERS, A TALE OF TRIUMPH WAITING TO BE WRITTEN, WITH ME AS ITS SCRIBE, CHRONICLING EACH DAY'S VICTORIES WITH INK FORGED FROM DEDICATION, SERVICE, AND AN UNWAVERING BELIEF IN THE BOUNDLESS POSSIBILITIES THAT EACH NEW DAWN BRINGS.

> *"Great leaders understand that accountability is the cornerstone of success, and they establish effective systems and processes to ensure everyone is on a journey toward excellence."*
> **—Glenn Lundy**

As the week continued Alfred began to notice the signs of spring were in the air. The trees were growing leaves, the air beginning to warm up, and the traffic in the store was beginning to increase as well.

Spring was tax season. A big season in the auto industry. People from far and wide would be getting tax returns that they would, in turn, use as down payments to buy new vehicles. Without fail, March was always the busiest month in the auto industry.

Knowing this was the case, Alfred thought this would be the perfect time to add another layer. He grabbed the chest from his safe, opened it up, and grabbed the next Title.

The Title Marked IV
The 8-5-3-1 Formula

As the golden tapestry of dawn unfolds across the sky, I unfurl the Title marked IV, allowing its wisdom to illuminate my path with the brilliance of the 8-5-3-1 Formula—a sacred sequence that whispers the secret rhythms of success.

With the first light of dawn, my journey begins. Eight leads, akin to the cardinal points on an ancient compass, shall serve as my guides through the vast seas of opportunity. These are not mere names or numbers but living, breathing entities with desires, hopes, and needs similar to my own. I shall approach each lead not as a conqueror but as a servant, offering assistance rather than insistence, and providing value that resonates with the symphony of their aspirations.

Out of the abundant eight, I shall carefully cultivate a garden of five appointments. These appointments are the bridges that connect the islands of opportunity, and it is my duty to ensure that these bridges are sturdy, welcoming, and actively used. Each appointment is a dance, a delicate ballet of giving and receiving, understanding, and explaining, listening, and speaking. With open ears and an open heart, I shall enter these appointments, sowing the seeds of trust and nurturing them with reliability and respect.

Yet, the Title sagely reminds me, not all seeds shall sprout, not all flowers shall bloom. Of the five appointments nurtured with care and commitment, three shall bear fruit. These three appointments that materialize into reality are precious, and I shall treat them as such—with respect, focus, and unparalleled service. Within the realm of these appointments, I shall not merely be a salesperson but a guide, an advisor, a consultant whose primary aim is to illuminate the path for the client, making their journey enjoyable, straightforward, and rewarding.

In the grand tapestry of the day, amidst the dance of appointments and the melody of leads, one car shall find its new owner. This is not just a transaction but a transformation—a moment where dreams are handed keys, aspirations settle into the driver's seat, and possibilities are ignited with the turn of an engine. Selling one car represents more than a financial gain; it signifies the blossoming of relationships, the establishment of trust, and the building of our dealership's legacy as a beacon of service and value.

The 8-5-3-1 Formula is not rigid, but fluid, adaptable to the ebbs and flows of the marketplace, responsive to the unique nuances of each client. Each number in this sacred sequence serves as a steppingstone, guiding me across the river of the day toward the shores of success, where the fruit of one car sold awaits, ripe and ready for harvest.

With the Title Marked IV clutched close to my heart, bearing the sacred 8-5-3-1 Formula inscribed upon it, I step forward into the day. My eyes are alight with purpose, my heart is brimming with a commitment to service. For within the numerical dance of eight leads, five appointments set, three appointments kept, and one car sold, lies the symphony of success—a melody of prosperity and fulfillment, not only for myself but for all who enter our hallowed dealership doors.

With the Title in hand, I advance, ready to embody and enact the sacred rhythm, the heartbeat of success: the 8-5-3-1 Formula. For within its simplicity lies unmatched power, within its numbers, a tale of triumph waiting to be written, with me as its scribe, chronicling each day's victories with ink forged from *dedication, service, and an unwavering belief in the boundless possibilities that each new dawn brings.*

Out of all the Titles, the 8-5-3-1 Formula scared Alfred the most. It was breaking down a straightforward process, but he was struggling to really wrap his brain around it. He jotted down a quick note; **Eight Leads. Five Appointments. Three Shows. One sold.** Then he asked Doreen to come join him in his office so he could maybe get some outside insight.

"Okay Doreen, so let me ask you a question. Do you think it's possible for a salesperson to sell one car a day, every day that they are at work?"

Without hesitation, Doreen replied "Yes."

Alfred was taken aback.

"Well… then… if it's possible, why is it every other dealership in America and the organizations that support them, all agree that ten to twelve cars sold a month per salesperson is a good job and what should be expected?" Alfred asked defiantly.

"Because everyone is going off the standard set back in the seventies. No one has adjusted for the times, and no one has taken the time to create an environment where it's not just possible, but expected, and in some cases actually easy, to do more," said Doreen.

Alfred looked at Doreen with a bit of astonishment. Doreen continued.

"Listen Alfred, there is a guy named John Maxwell who tells an amazing story about how he was at a holiday dinner with his extended family, and his wife was cooking a roast. He noticed she cut the end off the roast before she put it in the oven. Mr. Maxwell asked his wife why she did that, and she told him that it made the roast juicier, it made the roast taste better, and that her mother taught her to do it that way."

"This answer didn't sit well with John, so he went to his wife's mother who was also there for the holiday. He asked her the same question, and to his surprise she responded the same way, stating that it made the roast juicier, it made the roast taste better, and her mother had taught her to do it that way."

This still didn't sit well with John, so he went to his wife's mom's mom, who was also there for the holiday dinner. He asked her the same question and this time he got a different reply. She told John that when they were in the middle of the great depression they couldn't afford a big oven, so they bought a little one, and when she went to cook a roast, she would always have to cut the end off in order to make it fit.

"So, you see Alfred, things aren't always what they seem. **People just tend to do things the way they've always been done, and in most cases never question why.** I mean think about it, how is it possible that the expectations in our industry are the same when so many things have changed?"

"We now have the internet, social media, cell phones, video cameras, automatic approvals, laser printers and computers for goodness' sake! Every tool in the industry has changed, and yet the expectations of the people have stayed exactly the same. It doesn't make any sense, and if I'm being honest Alfred, I think it's kind of irresponsible of you, and other leaders like you, to allow people to continue performing at standards set decades ago," Doreen finished coyly.

"Irresponsible?! Of me?! Oh Doreen, please do tell." Alfred smirked.

"Gladly." Doreen sat up straight. "You have people who leave their families at 7:30 in the morning to show up for work at 8:30 A.M. Then they work all day until 8:00 P.M. and two out of three days they go home empty handed. No salary, no hourly pay, no nothing. They either sell a car and make money, or they don't.

"Now for years this company has been okay with that, because in the end, if each person sells ten to twelve cars a month the dealership usually ends up profitable. BUT that goes back to the thirty-day windows this industry constantly operates in, short-term thinking that keeps the business from growing. So, let me ask you, as the LEADER of this organization, do you not feel any responsibility to make sure your people are successful EVERY day? I mean, if they can make a decent living selling ten to twelve cars a month, what could they do for their families if they were selling twice that many? Isn't that what you want? For them to "Win the day!" and ultimately "Win" at life?" Doreen jabbed at the daily goal board hanging behind Alfred's head.

Alfred took a deep breath. The thing he loved most about Doreen is she always shot him straight. She never held back, and though he would never tell her to her face, she was usually right.

"I guess that's one way you can look at it." Alfred responded sheepishly, knowing good and well he couldn't combat a single thing Doreen just said. "So, let's just say you might be right. What if I told you I had an idea of how to make sure that happens. A way we could guarantee that every salesperson would be successful every day they walked into this building. Would you be willing to help me execute it?"

Doreen's eyes widened. "I'd be more than willing Alfred. I'd be honored."

Without divulging the origin of the 8-5-3-1 formula, Alfred began to break down his understanding of it, and mixed in some common language that he knew Doreen would understand.

"Okay, for starters, let's take a look at the "The Automotive Triangle"." He pulled out the image of the triangle he had received at an automotive workshop years earlier. On it was a triangle, with a label on each side. "Inventory" he said as he pointed. "Marketing" he gestured towards the other side, "and People and Processes." He noted was across the base of the triangle. "Every aspect of our business, and any other business for that matter falls under one of these three categories and ends up inside the business triangle.

INVENTORY

800%

PEOPLE & PROCESSES

MARKETING

Alfred put the picture of "The Automotive Triangle," on the table and then grabbed another sheet of paper and wrote in big numbers down the page from top to bottom "8-5-3-1". He then placed both pieces of paper next to each other.

"So these three things are what we have control over. We can control our used car inventory, utilizing auctions and whatnot, and outside of a pandemic, we can usually get a fairly good sense of what's happening with our new cars."

"Marketing is 800% under our control. We choose how we do it, who we work with, and how much we spend."

And lastly, "People and Processes," we determine what our process looks like, and we select the people who operate and manage those processes. Keeping all that in mind, I am curious if we can tie into these numbers on the right.

Now follow me here, if we can generate eight leads per salesperson per day, every day that they are at work, and then out of those eight leads get five people to set appointments with us, then as long as at least three of those appointments show up, one is guaranteed to buy a car." He looked up to Doreen and could see her mind spinning.

He continued to discuss the theory, and with additional insights from Doreen, began to formulate a plan on how they could bring it to reality.

First, they had to look at the numbers. They had 18 salespeople. The Title said that every eight leads should cultivate into a sale. So, if they wanted to guarantee one sale for every salesperson, every day, that meant they would need to do one of two things, either they had to generate 144 leads per day, or they had to cut back their sales staff to match their current number of leads.

Alfred didn't want to fire anyone, so it was going to require them to take a deep dive into their marketing budget. More leads were going to cost more money, unless, as Doreen pointed out, they could find a way to utilize organic social media better. Things like Facebook, TikTok, Instagram, etc., wouldn't cost them anything extra and they both knew of other businesses that had social media strategies that were amazingly effective.

Secondly, they had to look at the process of what actually happened once a lead was generated. It wouldn't matter how many leads they got per day if they couldn't convert those leads into appointments. Exactly as the Title described eight leads had to convert into five appointments, those appointments had to turn into three shows and those three shows guaranteed one sold.

They started breaking down their current lead process and quickly realized there was a lot of room for improvement. They had leads that were not getting responded to quickly enough and others that had responses, but the responses were sub-par. They had nearly zero follow-up if the lead wasn't contacted quickly, and after listening to some calls they were able to understand why people would choose not to set an appointment. There was a lot of training that needed to be done.

Of course, that then took them to the next step in the process, which was how do they make sure the appointments they have actually show up?

Again, they went to look at their current process. It was a short journey because…well because…if they were honest, they didn't really have a process in place in which to look at. For years it had always been the same: appointments got set, appointments got logged, and then everyone sat back and hoped the appointment would show up.

Nowhere in their current process were they even tracking the number of people who actually showed up vs. the ones who committed to doing so. Alfred was actually a bit embarrassed he'd let the business run this way for so long.

They moved on to the next part of the formula. Doreen and Alfred agreed that no matter what, if a salesperson talked to at least three customers face-to-face throughout the day, he, or she for sure would sell at least one. They actually had data that clearly supported this, and in fact, the current numbers were that two out of three people bought once they made it into the store, not just one. So, one out of three was a no brainer.

After analyzing everything, it became clear that this was not going to be an easy undertaking. There was training that would have to take place, budgets moved around, and new systems and processes developed. It was going to take months, if not longer, to get everything in place.

Alfred's current paid marketing strategy had to be completely upended. He was spending money in eleven separate places for advertising, and it turned out when he really looked at it, there were actually just three sources that were generating leads way cheaper than all the others. Google SEO/SEM, FB Carousel Ads, and AutoTrader were driving traffic at a low enough cost per lead that maybe, just maybe, Alfred could afford to invest enough capital to get close to the 8-5-3-1 formula's requirements.

It would be tight though, and it became clear that Smith Chevrolet couldn't be guaranteed to get there with paid marketing alone. He was going to need his people to contribute as well.

Alfred was utterly amazed at how such a simple little formula could affect so many aspects of his business. From marketing strategies to systems and processes, and now it had him thinking about ways to better train his people. It was spectacular really.

The thing he had to tackle now was how he could get his people trained to utilize social media to drive in new leads. He did a bunch of research on social media and came across Glenn Lundy again. Glenn had posted a video teaching exactly how to gain traction, build a community, and drive leads through social media. Alfred was elated to find it, and even more excited to see how easy it was. He studied the video, took notes, and determined he would immediately start using the daily meetings to train the team on what Glenn called "The Four "Ps" of social media.

The Four "Ps" of Social Media

Personal Post – This is a post that you make that can be anything about you as a person. Hobbies, likes, family, travel, etc. Anything about you as a person, not you as a business or a professional.

Professional Post – This is a post about you as a business or a professional. This post should tell whoever comes across it what you do, and how you do it better than anyone else. This is your opportunity to brag about what makes you unique and why someone should do business with you. Have fun with it, and don't hold back.

Purposeful Post – With this post I want you to make the reader feel something. Something POSITIVE. No politics, controversial topics, or negativity. Make me laugh. Make me cry happy tears. Inspire me. Motivate me. Educate me. Use a picture, or a meme, or a video. Whatever it is, just make sure I feel it; that's what is most important.

Poll - This post is amazingly simple. Just ask a question. Any question. Understand this though, the question needs to be at the beginning of the post, not after you write some long narrative, and the question should not be more than one sentence long. Also, people should be able to answer the question in one or two words. Here is a perfect example of a question that ultimately created the most viral post in social media history: "What color is this dress?" That's the format your question should be in and can be about anything at all. It doesn't have to be related to you or your business in any way. It's just there to connect with your audience and drive engagement.

Make two posts a day, following the order of Personal Post, Professional Post, Purposeful Post, and Poll. This will create a natural cycle to build a relationship online with your audience/potential clients.

We build relationships in real life the same way. We meet over something we share personally, like a church, or a gym, or a show that we like, a class, whatever. Then the first thing we ask when we meet people is; What do YOU do for a living? Then we share a laugh, or some valuable information, and this cements the value of this new person in our lives. Then we start asking lots of questions! "Where are you from? Do you have any kids? Who is your favorite President?" Just kidding. You don't want to start a new relationship with that last one.

This is how people can build a relationship with you online, as well as the trust you need in order for them to want to do business with you. Two posts a day, every day. Follow the process.

Alfred understood it wouldn't be easy at first, but at least with a simple formula like "The Four "P's," over time, he believed he could get everyone on board. He was also positive it would make a significant difference, both for the individuals, and for the store. It had to. Any action along these lines was better than no action at all.

This triggered a thought in Alfred. He was starting to realize that easy to use systems and processes really made a profound difference in the long run. In the past, he had sometimes felt that holding himself and others around him accountable to some sort of structure would take away from the business' ability to adapt, evolve, or stay relevant. The reality was, *not* having a system just ends up creating chaos. Not to mention it is impossible to train on a subject, or duplicate results, without a simple, easy to understand, step-by-step process in place.

Alfred made a mental note to make sure every aspect of his dealership's operations had step-by-step, easy to understand, written processes in place. He understood it would take a while to get them all, but it was clearly important.

This brought Alfred back to the 8-5-3-1 formula. Though just four little, tiny numbers, this formula had the potential to become the backbone of the entire company.

CHAPTER 12
THE SUCCESS FORMULA

*"Efficiency is Doing Better
what is Already Being Done."*
—Peter Drucker

Over the next couple of months, Alfred made the changes he needed to in both his marketing and his sales staff. Creating an environment where he was now driving six leads per salesperson per day, and the salespeople themselves were using social media to drive the other two per day. eight total. This had taken a substantial number of tweaks to his advertising budget, his advertising agency strategies, and his inventory, and dozens of hours of social media training.

One thing that he had found really interesting along the way, was that for decades Smith Chevrolet carried primarily domestic used vehicles like Chevy, Ford, and Dodge, but after doing a lot of digging it turned out that in order to drive enough traffic for the 8-5-3-1 formula, they had to expand their inventory to foreign vehicles like Nissans, Hondas and Toyotas, causing him to get really dialed in on exactly what consumers were looking for online.

The right makes, the right models, the right mileage, and trim levels. All these things, including the colors of the vehicles, played a significant role in making the formula work. Without the right inventory, generating the amount of leads he needed was impossible.

In doing his research he was absolutely floored when he really dug into the data and found that 80% of consumers buy vehicles that are black, white, or silver, or some variant of black, white, or silver, like "Icelandic White" or "Midnight Black".

Finding this out alone was a huge revelation because Alfred couldn't tell you how many times he bought a red car, or a blue S.U.V. because it was a great price, only to have that vehicle sit on his lot for six months or more!

If he was being honest with himself, there was a small piece of Alfred that felt like an idiot for not noticing this before. But once he saw it, he couldn't unsee it. Every time he pulled into a parking lot, he couldn't help but notice 80% or more of the vehicles in that lot were black, white, or silver.

While he was sitting at a stoplight, the cars around him were black, white, or silver.

Driving down the interstate…nearly every vehicle he saw, black, white, or silver.

It was so clear everywhere, and yet for his entire life, Alfred had never seen it.

Also, while researching, he was able to determine that nearly 75% of online searches for used vehicles were for mid-size sedans and smaller S.U.V.'s priced between $19,000 and $27,000. This was in stark contrast to the inventory he was carrying, which was generally higher priced vehicles, or vehicles less than $15,000. More than 80% of his inventory actually fell *outside* of what most people were searching for…crazy.

Keeping up with all of this, however, had become a full-time job for Alfred, so he decided he had to hire someone specifically just to buy inventory. Just the thought of this alone was another revelation for Smith Chevrolet.

For fifty years now, the buying of used cars has always been done by a sales manager. Looking at it through this new lens of the Titles, Alfred could now see how foolish this was. Used cars were part of the lifeblood of his dealership, and yet they had been treating them like some part-time thing that could be done in between leading people, working deals, and all the other roles a sales manager had on his plate. Asking them to buy cars all day too? Ridiculous.

He hired a woman named Tina, and made it clear she had exactly one job: buy cars. That's it. And more specifically, to buy as close to an exact replica of any car Alfred's team had sold the day before, and then to look for black, white, and silver mid-size sedans and small S.U.V's that could be priced between $19,000 and $27,000. At least 75% of the overall inventory should match that, considering that's what 75% of people are looking for.

So once Alfred had the marketing in place, and over time had acquired the inventory to match what people were looking for, sales began to climb substantially. Leads were pouring in far beyond anything Smith Chevrolet had ever experienced, leading Alfred to now take a deeper look at the "5" in the 8-5-3-1 formula.

"Eight leads *should* equal five appointments. "Alfred said aloud to Doreen. "Right now, eight leads are converting at about three appointments. Well below the mark, thoughts?"

"Why five appointments?" questioned Doreen. "Why not four or six. Why five?

"Well…," Alfred fumbled around a bit. He wasn't comfortable mentioning the Titles to Doreen, so instead he decided to use data. "The data in the auto industry shows that you should be converting roughly 62% of leads into appointments. Five appointments hits that mark."

"Ah…Got it." Doreen retorted. "So, we're back doing that thing where we just accept whatever the standard in our industry *has* been?"

Alfred looked at her. He so appreciated how she often fired at him in a way that made him think creatively. "You're right, Doreen. I think the conversions could be even higher, but for now, let's use 62% and then as people get better trained and accustomed to handling objections better, that number can go up."

"The key, "Alfred continued "Is that we establish a baseline and stick to it. Anything less than five appointments per eight leads is not just unacceptable, it is considered detrimental to the business. With that being the case, what are the factors that determine whether or not we hit the target?"

"I would say the most important things are the speed of the response, the professionalism of the response, and the thoroughness of the response. Customers want what they want, and they want it now. If the response is slow, or sub-par, or it doesn't really address what they're asking for, then they likely won't set an appointment to come in," Doreen thoughtfully added.

"Correct." stated Alfred. "And if we look at our current process, it is none of those things. We have salespeople responding when they're available, with minimum thought going into it, and literally trying *not* to give customers information over the phone. All of that must change. **We need dedicated sales professionals who have one job and one job only: Give customers the information they need to be able to make a decision without ever putting them on hold.** It's as simple as that. We build that, and I'm positive we can get our appointments up over 62%."

They went to work doing just that. Scouring through their current sales team, they found a couple of individuals they thought were very professional, organized, well-spoken, and sounded pleasant on the phone. These people became their new "Front Line Sales Reps" with one extremely easy to understand job: **Give the customers the information they need to be able to make a decision without ever putting them on hold.**

This required these reps to train just like any other salesperson on the floor. They were a part of every daily meeting, they got paid commissions just like the salespeople in the showroom, and over time, became an integral, yet structurally different, part of the sales team. As they became more proficient at the role, it was only a matter of time before Smith Chevrolet was setting appointments consistently above 62%.

Alfred was on a roll.

Now he had to make sure those appointments showed up.

This part of the equation was much easier than Alfred had thought it would be. The Front-Line Sales Reps were doing such a fantastic job with their customers that people were actually excited to come in.

The Front-Line Sales Reps had also developed a process where they would put appointments on people's google calendars. Then they would follow up with them the day before their appointment, and then again, the morning of their appointment. They took a page from the dentist and doctor's handbook, making sure the customer did not lose sight of their appointment, and felt compelled to be on time.

Overall, three out of five customers who made appointments showed up for them, and in a lot of cases even four or five would show up. It really was spectacular to witness. Everyone in the dealership now knew the formula and worked diligently daily to make sure to reach or exceed its expectations.

Eight leads. Five Appointments. Three Shows. One sold.

The best part of the equation was that Alfred literally didn't have to do anything to achieve the final result. Once a customer had gone from being a lead, to setting an appointment, to showing up, the rest was easy. All they had to do was exactly what they'd been doing for 50 years. The thing they knew best how to do.

All they had to do is simply sell the car, and not screw it up.

The customer was there to buy. No one goes and hangs out at a dealership just to hang out. (Well almost no one, Alfred did have one off-duty police officer that would just hang out at the store all the time for some odd reason.) The people that were there had a need, or a desire, and they were ready to do business if Alfred and his team could make it happen.

And make it happen they did. It had now been two years since Alfred got the Titles, and in the month of October, Smith Chevrolet, for the first time ever, sold over 300 cars.

CHAPTER 13

FISCHER WENT PEE-PEE IN THE POTTY

> *"You can make more friends in two months*
> *by becoming interested in other people*
> *than you can in two years by trying to get*
> *other people interested in you."*
> —Dale Carnegie

They had a massive celebration. Alfred brought in a catered breakfast for the morning meeting and had his CFO give him $10,000 in cash. He started the morning meeting the same way by being the first one in the room, and with powerful positive music blaring, but this time as people came into the room, he was handing them hundred-dollar bills.

The energy was electric and once Alfred started going over all the positive things his team had done in October, he made sure to hand out stacks of cash with each accolade. "Brian! Get up here! Amazing job last month and I saw you working with one of the new hires yesterday. Keep up the magnificent work and here's an extra couple hundred bucks to start off your month!" Everyone clapped and celebrated.

It was a bit euphoric. Alfred and his team were doing things far beyond his wildest imagination. Sales were up, customers were happy, profits were at an all-time-high, and then…Doreen threatened to quit.

"Things are just different," Doreen explained. "It's like, no matter how many we sell, or how well we perform, you're always pushing for more. When is enough, enough Alfred? I personally am starting to feel like I'm just a number to you. A pawn in some game you're playing. I mean don't get me wrong, I am all for us breaking records, and celebrating, and I'm making more money than ever, but the money alone isn't why I've been with you all these years, it used to be so much more than that."

Alfred was floored. He couldn't believe his ears. Doreen was his closest confidant in the dealership, and someone he relied on heavily, not just to run the business, but to also keep him on track when necessary.

"Doreen, I'm admittedly surprised by this. I never imagined…I mean, can you give me some time to process all of this? You are tremendously valuable to me and this company, and I appreciate you sharing how you feel. I just need a bit to wrap my head around it. Cool?" Alfred peered deeply into Doreen's eyes. She could tell he was sincere.

"Sure Alfred, we can talk later." Doreen replied. "Thanks." She then turned around and walked out of Alfreds office.

Alfred immediately grabbed the chest. There had to be something in the Titles that could help him understand and rectify this.

To his surprise he didn't find just one that fit the situation he found that the next three all pointed to his people.

The Title Marked V "Make People Feel Special, Feel Important, and Like They're the Only One." The Title Marked VI "Build a Family." And The Title Marked VII "Be a Servant Leader"

It seemed there were aspects to all three of these Titles that fed into the situation with Doreen, and if Alfred was honest, he knew there had to be other people that felt the same way Doreen did.

Alfred read The Title Marked V, one more time:

Title V

- CERTIFICATE OF TITLE NUMBER V -

MAKE PEOPLE FEEL SPECIAL
FEEL IMPORTANT
AND LIKE THEY'RE THE ONLY ONE

BEHOLD, IN MY HAND, I CLUTCH THE GOLDEN KEY TO TRANSCENDENT SERVICE AND BOUNDLESS SUCCESS. IT IS A TRUTH BOTH SIMPLE AND INFINITELY POWERFUL: "MAKE PEOPLE FEEL SPECIAL, FEEL IMPORTANT, AND LIKE THEY'RE THE ONLY ONE." THIS SHALL BE MY GUIDING STAR, CASTING LIGHT UPON THE PATH TO DEEP CONNECTIONS AND UNWAVERING LOYALTY.

AS THE SUN GENTLY KISSES THE EARTH WITH ITS FIRST RAYS, BESTOWING WARMTH, AND LIFE UPON ALL IT TOUCHES, SO SHALL I BESTOW UPON EVERY SOUL I ENCOUNTER THE PRECIOUS GIFTS OF RECOGNITION AND VALUE. WITH EYES THAT TRULY SEE, EARS THAT ATTENTIVELY LISTEN, AND A HEART THAT DEEPLY UNDERSTANDS, I SHALL ACKNOWLEDGE THE UNIQUE ESSENCE OF EACH INDIVIDUAL. FOR IN THE VAST TAPESTRY OF HUMANITY, EVERY THREAD IS INDISPENSABLE.

WHEN A CUSTOMER STANDS BEFORE ME, THEY SHALL NOT STAND ALONE. THEY SHALL STAND BATHED IN THE SPOTLIGHT OF MY UNDIVIDED ATTENTION, SHIELDED FROM THE SHADOWS OF NEGLECT AND INDIFFERENCE. THEIR VOICE SHALL NOT DISSIPATE INTO THE VOID BUT RESONATE WITHIN THE CHAMBERS OF MY MIND, CARRYING WITH IT STORIES OF NEEDS, DESIRES, AND DREAMS THAT ONLY I CAN FULFILL.

TO MAKE ONE FEEL SPECIAL IS NOT TO WEAVE ILLUSIONS OF GRANDEUR BUT TO REVEAL THE TRUTH THAT OFTEN LIES HIDDEN BENEATH LAYERS OF DOUBT AND INVISIBILITY. THROUGH MY WORDS, MY ACTIONS, THE TIMBRE OF MY VOICE, AND THE LIGHT IN MY EYES, I SHALL CONVEY, "YOU MATTER. YOU ARE SEEN. YOU ARE UNIQUE, AND IN YOUR UNIQUENESS, YOU ARE IRREPLACEABLE."

TO **MAKE** ONE FEEL IMPORTANT IS TO PLACE THE CROWN OF DIGNITY UPON THEIR HEAD, ACKNOWLEDGING THEIR WORTH AND CONTRIBUTIONS TO THE GRAND SYMPHONY OF LIFE. WITH GRATITUDE AND RESPECT, I SHALL TREAT EACH PERSON NOT AS A MERE COG IN THE MACHINE BUT AS AN ARCHITECT OF DESTINY, A BEARER OF WISDOM, AND A HOLDER OF THE KEY TO UNTOLD POSSIBILITIES.

TO MAKE ONE FEEL LIKE THEY'RE THE ONLY ONE IS TO CRAFT AN OASIS OF CONNECTION AMIDST THE DESERT OF ALIENATION. IN THE SACRED SPACE BETWEEN WORDS AND SILENCE, GESTURES AND STILLNESS, I SHALL CONSTRUCT A BRIDGE OF UNDERSTANDING—AN UNSPOKEN PACT OF TRUST AND RELIABILITY THAT SHALL WITHSTAND THE TESTS OF TIME AND CIRCUMSTANCE.

BY THIS PRINCIPLE, I SHALL LIVE, AND BY THIS PRINCIPLE, I SHALL THRIVE. IN THE GARDEN OF HUMAN RELATIONSHIPS, I SHALL BE THE DILIGENT GARDENER, NURTURING THE BLOSSOMS OF SELF-WORTH AND BELONGING WITH THE WATERS OF ACKNOWLEDGMENT AND THE SUNLIGHT OF APPRECIATION. AND AS I GIVE, SO SHALL I RECEIVE, FOR IN THE MIRROR OF LIFE, THE REFLECTION OF LOVE AND RESPECT SHINES BRIGHTEST WHEN IT EMANATES FROM WITHIN.

THIS IS THE TITLE MARKED V, AND WITH ITS WISDOM ETCHED UPON MY HEART, I SHALL STEP FORTH INTO THE DAWN OF A NEW DAY, BEARING THE TORCH OF EXCEPTIONAL SERVICE AND UNYIELDING COMMITMENT TO THE CELEBRATION OF HUMANITY IN ALL ITS GLORIOUS DIVERSITY. THROUGH THIS, I SHALL NOT ONLY BE A SUCCESSFUL SALESPERSON BUT ALSO A BEACON OF LIGHT AND INSPIRATION TO ALL WHO CROSS MY PATH.

The Title Marked V

*Make People Feel Special, Feel Important,
and Like They're the Only One.*

Behold, in my hand, I clutch the golden key to transcendent service and boundless success. It is a truth both simple and infinitely powerful: "Make People Feel Special, Feel Important, and Like They're the Only One." This shall be my guiding star, casting light upon the path to deep connections and unwavering loyalty.

As the sun gently kisses the earth with its first rays, bestowing warmth, and life upon all it touches, so shall I bestow upon every soul I encounter the precious gifts of recognition and value. With eyes that truly see, ears that attentively listen, and a heart that deeply understands, I shall acknowledge the unique essence of each individual. For in the vast tapestry of humanity, every thread is indispensable.

When a customer stands before me, they shall not stand alone. They shall stand bathed in the spotlight of my undivided attention, shielded from the shadows of neglect and indifference. Their voice shall not dissipate into the void but resonate within the chambers of my mind, carrying with it stories of needs, desires, and dreams that only I can fulfill.

To make one feel special is not to weave illusions of grandeur but to reveal the truth that often lies hidden beneath layers of doubt and invisibility. Through my words, my actions, the timbre of my voice, and the light in my eyes, I shall convey, "You matter. You are seen. You are unique, and in your uniqueness, you are irreplaceable."

To make one feel important is to place the crown of dignity upon their head, acknowledging their worth and contributions to the grand symphony of life. With gratitude and respect, I shall treat each person not as a mere cog in the machine but as an architect of destiny, a bearer of wisdom, and a holder of the key to untold possibilities.

To make one feel like they're the only one is to craft an oasis of connection amidst the desert of alienation. In the sacred space between words and silence, gestures, and stillness, I shall construct a bridge of understanding—an unspoken pact of trust and reliability that shall withstand the tests of time and circumstance.

By this principle, I shall live, and by this principle, I shall thrive. In the garden of human relationships, I shall be the diligent gardener, nurturing the blossoms of self-worth and belonging with the waters of acknowledgment and the sunlight of appreciation. And as I give, so shall I receive, for in the mirror of life, the reflection of love and respect shines brightest when it emanates from within.

This is the Title Marked V, and with its wisdom etched upon my heart, I shall step forth into the dawn of a new day, bearing the torch of exceptional service and unyielding commitment to the celebration of humanity in all its glorious diversity. Through this, I shall not only be a successful salesperson but also a beacon of light and inspiration to all who cross my path.

Alfred immediately thought about his most recent customer interaction. He literally had his phone to his ear, while talking to a customer in person about their transaction in his service department. All he wanted to do was get out of that conversation, and so he insisted that he would take care of them, but he needed to finish his phone call first.

He then began to think about how many times he's done this with his staff, his kids, his wife. Clearly this was a problem he was going to have to remedy quickly, and the more he contemplated, he decided he probably owed quite a few people an apology as well.

He then went back and re-read the Title one more time. The exquisite way it laid out how to interact with others resonated deeply within Alfred's soul. **"Through my words, my actions, the timbre of my voice, and the light in my eyes, I shall convey, "You matter. You are seen. You are unique, and in your uniqueness, you are irreplaceable."**

When it came to interactions with customers, Alfred believed he did almost everything in the Title. (Except the times he was on his phone.) He always made the customer the number one priority. His meetings always got pushed to the side if a customer needed something, anything at all, and when possible, Alfred made sure they had his undivided attention. As far as he was concerned, he did an excellent job of making people feel special, important, and like they were the only one. As a matter of fact, he didn't just make people feel that way, but in his mind, they *were* special, they *were* important, and they *were* the only ones.

That's how Alfred had been raised. The customer is always right; the customer deserves your undivided attention; the customer is the lifeblood of the dealership.

BUT…Alfred was learning that just because that's the way things have always been, that doesn't mean it's true.

He started to analyze the whole picture. Each day Alfred would come to work and celebrate his team. Then he would dive into his day, meeting with vendors, handling any upset customers, solving problems, analyzing data, mapping out ads and commercials, responding to customer reviews, answering emails, voicemails, and text messages, meeting with leadership, interviewing potential salespeople, and on and on and on. Alfred spent at least 80% of his day in his office…At least. The only times he came out were to check in on the sales numbers for the day, grab a bite to eat, or to meet with someone about a potential new product, gadget, or widget for their store.

Outside of the daily morning meeting, Alfred's team was last on the priority list. Not last because he didn't care, but last because that's just simply where they landed at the end of the day.

Alfred's team members had regretfully become the people in his life he took most for granted. The Title made it clear. Did his customers feel special? Usually. But did his people? That question he wasn't sure he wanted to answer.

He went on to read the next of the three Titles associated with his people:

Title VI

- CERTIFICATE OF TITLE NUMBER VI -

BUILD A FAMILY

BEHOLD, AS THIS TITLE UNFURLS, IT REVEALS A SECRET, SUBTLE YET POTENT, WHICH BINDS HEARTS TOGETHER IN A TAPESTRY SO TIGHT AND ENDURING THAT IT CAN WITHSTAND ANY TEMPEST. "BUILD A FAMILY," IT WHISPERS SOFTLY, NOT OF BLOOD BUT OF SPIRIT: NOT OF LINEAGE BUT OF SHARED PURPOSE AND UNWAVERING COMMITMENT.

WITHIN THE SACRED HALLS WHERE COMMERCE UNFOLDS, AND THE DANCE OF TRADE TAKES ITS COURSE, LIES AN OPPORTUNITY-A CHANCE TO FORGE BONDS AS STEADFAST AND NURTURING AS THOSE OF KIN. WHEN A PERSON ENTERS MY REALM, EAGER TO ENGAGE IN BUSINESS, THEY SHALL NOT ENCOUNTER A STRANGER, COLD AND CALCULATING. INSTEAD, THEY SHALL BE WELCOMED BY A FAMILIAR AND COMFORTING PRESENCE, ONE THAT EMANATES THE WARMTH OF FAMILY.

IN THE PURSUIT OF PROFIT, THE ALLURE OF NUMBERS AND THE GLEAM OF GOLD MAY SOMETIMES BEDAZZLE AND ENCHANT THE MIND. YET, LET ME NOT FORGET THAT BEHIND EACH TRANSACTION, EACH NEGOTIATION, STANDS A HUMAN BEING WITH DREAMS AKIN TO MINE, WITH HOPES THAT FLUTTER AND SOAR IN THE BOUNDLESS SKY. AS I EXTEND MY HAND, OFFERING NOT JUST A PRODUCT BUT AN EXPERIENCE STEEPED IN CARE AND UNDERSTANDING, I EXTEND AN INVITATION TO JOIN A CIRCLE, A FAMILY BORN NOT OF NECESSITY, BUT OF CHOICE AND TRUST.

BUT HOW DOES ONE BUILD A FAMILY AMIDST THE EBB AND FLOW OF BUSINESS? IT BEGINS WITH EYES THAT SEE BELOW THE SURFACE, PEELING BACK THE LAYERS TO ACKNOWLEDGE THE HUMANITY BENEATH. IT INVOLVES EARS THAT LISTEN NOT JUST TO THE SPOKEN WORD, BUT TO THE SYMPHONY OF EMOTIONS AND THOUGHTS THAT LINGER IN THE SILENT SPACES BETWEEN. IT REQUIRES A HEART THAT IS OPEN AND GENEROUS, READY TO GIVE WITHOUT COUNTING THE COST, AND TO SUPPORT WITHOUT MEASURING THE WEIGHT.

AS THE DAWN KISSES THE HORIZON, USHERING IN A NEW DAY, I SHALL RISE WITH A RESOLVE TEMPERED IN THE FIRES OF LOVE AND CAMARADERIE. EACH MEMBER OF MY TEAM, MY FAMILY, SHALL EXPERIENCE THE POWER OF BELONGING, THE STRENGTH THAT ARISES FROM KNOWING THAT IN LIFE'S ARENA, THEY DO NOT STAND ALONE. TOGETHER, WE SHALL CELEBRATE VICTORIES, NO MATTER HOW SMALL. TOGETHER, WE SHALL NAVIGATE THROUGH STORMS, NO MATTER HOW FIERCE.

IN THE RADIANCE OF FAMILY, THE COLD FACADE OF BUSINESS SHALL TRANSFORM INTO A HOME-A PLACE WHERE LAUGHTER RESONATES AND SUPPORT FLOWS, WHERE EACH INDIVIDUAL, REGARDLESS OF THEIR ROLE, FEELS SEEN, VALUED, AND ESSENTIAL TO THE TAPESTRY WE WEAVE TOGETHER. WITH THE THREADS OF RESPECT, EMPATHY, AND GENUINE CARE, THE FABRIC OF FAMILY SHALL BE WOVEN, PROVIDING A BACKDROP AGAINST WHICH THE DANCE OF COMMERCE BECOMES A CELEBRATION OF CONNECTION AND SHARED TRIUMPH.

WITH THE WISDOM OF TITLE MARKED VI ETCHED INTO MY SOUL, I SHALL MOVE FORWARD, NOT AS A LONE WANDERER BUT AS A MEMBER OF A CARAVAN-VIBRANT AND DYNAMIC, BOUND TOGETHER BY INVISIBLE THREADS OF LOVE AND UNWAVERING COMMITMENT, JOURNEYING TOWARD BRIGHT AND PROMISING HORIZONS.

The Title Marked VI

Build a Family

Behold, as this Title unfurls, it reveals a secret, subtle yet potent, which binds hearts together in a tapestry so tight and enduring that it can withstand any tempest. "Build a Family," it whispers softly, not of blood but of spirit; not of lineage but of shared purpose and unwavering commitment.

Within the sacred halls where commerce unfolds, and the dance of trade takes its course, lies an opportunity—a chance to forge bonds as steadfast and nurturing as those of kin. When a person enters my realm, eager to engage in business, they shall not encounter a stranger, cold and calculating. Instead, they shall be welcomed by a familiar and comforting presence, one that emanates the warmth of family.

In the pursuit of profit, the allure of numbers and the gleam of gold may sometimes bedazzle and enchant the mind. Yet, let me not forget that behind each transaction, each negotiation, stands a human being with dreams akin to mine, with hopes that flutter and soar in the boundless sky. As I extend my hand, offering not just a product but an experience steeped in care and understanding, I create an invitation to join a circle, a family born not of necessity, but of choice and trust.

But how does one build a family amidst the ebb and flow of business? It begins with eyes that see below the surface, peeling back the layers to acknowledge the humanity beneath. It involves ears that listen not just to the spoken word, but to the symphony of emotions and thoughts that linger in the silent spaces between. It requires a heart that is open and generous, ready to give without counting the cost, and to support without measuring the weight.

As the dawn kisses the horizon, ushering in a new day, I shall rise with a resolve tempered in the fires of love and camaraderie. Each member of my team, my family, shall experience the power of belonging, the strength that arises from knowing that in life's arena, they do not stand alone. Together, we shall celebrate *victories, no matter how small. Together, we shall navigate through storms, no matter how fierce.*

In the radiance of family, the cold facade of business shall transform into a home—a place where laughter resonates and support flows, where each individual, regardless of their role, feels seen, valued, and essential to the tapestry we weave together. With the threads of respect, empathy, and genuine care, the fabric of family shall be woven, providing a backdrop against which the dance of commerce becomes a celebration of connection and shared triumph.

With the wisdom of Title Marked VI etched into my soul, I shall move forward, not as a lone wanderer but as a member of a caravan—vibrant and dynamic, bound together by invisible threads of love and unwavering commitment, journeying toward bright and promising horizons.

Okay, now Alfred was starting to get upset. This was absolutely contrary to everything he had been taught by some of his dealer friends.

"Leave home at home, and work at work," he'd been taught.

"It's not a family, it's a business," he'd been told repeatedly.

But as he thought back to the people who gave him that advice, he realized that those people had all reached roughly the same level of success as he had prior to his grandfather's passing.

"Just because everyone else is doing it, doesn't mean it's the right thing to do." Alfred thought.

In truth, the entire Title was profound, but there was one sentence that really stood out – "a place where laughter resonates and support flows, where each individual, regardless of their role, feels seen, valued, and essential to the tapestry we weave together."

Alfred thought back to the time him, and Betty had gone to the Vatican in Rome. They walked through the halls of the tremendous Catholic church in awe of the statues, artifacts, and the paintings on the walls, but it was when they walked down the hall of tapestries that Alfred remembered most.

He and Betty had come around a corner and began to walk down this seemingly endless hall of tapestries. Gazing at their astounding beauty, he began to have an emotional experience. With each step down the hall, tears literally began to well up in his eyes. He was moved by their exquisite design. He stared at each huge work of art, woven together painstakingly, one ink-stained thread at a time, absolutely blown away by the intention and mindfulness that each tapestry held.

Alfred had never seen anything like the tapestries before in his life, and now in this moment, as he sat here thinking about his team, he had to come to grips with the fact that those tapestries, woven together thousands of years ago, had received far more intention, and attention than the dynamics of his team ever had.

Instead of an extremely precise work of art, Alfred had thrown together a hodge podge of individuals and simply demanded them to follow his processes and his lead. There hadn't been much thought around the tapestry of his culture at all, and it was becoming increasingly clear why Doreen wasn't seeing the impactful beauty in what they had built and were trying to expand upon.

Alfred then began to read the last of the three Titles he believed might help him with Doreen.

Title VII

- CERTIFICATE OF TITLE NUMBER VII -

BE A SERVANT LEADER

AS THE FIRST LIGHT OF DAWN GENTLY KISSES THE EARTH, I BEGIN MY DAY WITH A NOBLE RESOLUTION - TO BE A SERVANT UNTO OTHERS, FOR IN SERVICE, I SHALL FIND THE TRUE ESSENCE OF LEADERSHIP.

I SHALL DON THE MANTLE OF HUMILITY AS I MOVE THROUGH THE DAY, RECOGNIZING THAT EACH SOUL I ENCOUNTER IS ENDOWED WITH DREAMS AND HOPES JUST AS VIBRANT AND WORTHY AS MY OWN. IN THE ECHOING SILENCE OF MY HEART, A SOLEMN VOW RESONATES, COMMITTING ME TO UPLIFT, SUPPORT, AND NURTURE, ACTING AS THE GENTLE WIND BENEATH THE WINGS OF THOSE IN MY CHARGE.

YES, A SERVANT LEADER IS THE VISAGE I SHALL PRESENT TO THE WORLD. POWER AND CONTROL, THOUGH TEMPTING, SHALL NOT BEGUILE ME INTO THEIR INTOXICATING EMBRACE. FOR TRUE LEADERSHIP WHISPERS, IT DOES NOT SHOUT: SUPPORTS IT DOES NOT SUPPRESS: AND IT ILLUMINATES, NEVER OVERSHADOWS.

MY EARS SHALL BE SANCTUARIES OF UNDERSTANDING, ALWAYS OPEN, EVER RECEPTIVE TO THE SYMPHONIES AND SOLILOQUIES OF THOSE I LEAD. THEIR CONCERNS SHALL NOT FALL ON BARREN GROUND BUT SHALL BE SEEDED WITHIN THE FERTILE SOIL OF MY CONSCIOUSNESS, TENDED WITH CARE AND CONSIDERATION.

WITH HANDS EXTENDED, NOT TO TAKE, BUT TO GIVE, I SHALL BE A BEACON OF SUPPORT AND ENCOURAGEMENT. IN TIMES OF TRIUMPH, MINE SHALL BE THE SOFT CLAP IN THE CHORUS OF ACCOLADES, GENTLY PUSHING THEM TO BASK IN THE SPOTLIGHT THEY HAVE EARNED. IN TIMES OF TRIBULATION, MINE SHALL BE THE SHOULDER OFFERED, THE SILENT STRENGTH UPON WHICH THEY CAN LEAN WITHOUT FEAR OR HESITATION.

EYES, CLEAR AND UNCLOUDED BY THE MIST OF ARROGANCE, SHALL SEE BEYOND THE VEIL OF TITLES AND POSITIONS, PERCEIVING THE IRREPLACEABLE VALUE OF EACH INDIVIDUAL. NO TASK SHALL BE DEEMED TOO MENIAL, NO ROLE INSIGNIFICANT, FOR IN THE GRAND TAPESTRY OF SUCCESS, EVERY THREAD HOLDS IMPORTANCE, EVERY COLOR CONTRIBUTES TO THE MASTERPIECE.

WITH EACH DAWN, I SHALL BE REBORN, RENEWED IN MY VOW TO BE A SERVANT LEADER. WITH A SPIRIT UNBURDENED BY THE WEIGHT OF EGO, I SHALL LEAD BY EXAMPLE, LIVING THE PRINCIPLES I ESPOUSE, EMBODYING THE VALUES I CHAMPION.

THROUGH THE EBB AND FLOW OF THE DAY, THROUGH THE CYCLE OF SEASONS, IN MOMENTS OF UNCERTAINTY AND EPOCHS OF CLARITY, THIS TITLE SHALL BE MY COMPASS, GUIDING ME GENTLY TOWARDS THE ZENITH OF SERVANT LEADERSHIP. FOR IN SERVING, I LEAD, AND IN LEADING, I SERVE, COMPLETING THE CIRCLE OF INFLUENCE AND IMPACT, WEAVING A LEGACY OF INSPIRATION FOR GENERATIONS YET UNBORN.

SO, WITH THE FIRST RAY OF SUNLIGHT CASTING ITS GLOW UPON THE CANVAS OF THE DAY, I STEP FORTH, TITLE MARKED SEVEN IN HAND, HEART ALIGNED WITH THE TIMELESS PRINCIPLE ETCHED UPON ITS SURFACE: BE A SERVANT LEADER. AND AS THE SUN SETS, BATHING THE SKY IN HUES OF GOLD AND CRIMSON, I SHALL REST, KNOWING THAT IN SERVICE, I HAVE TRULY LED, AND IN LEADERSHIP, I HAVE GENUINELY SERVED.

The Title Marked VII

Be A Servant Leader

As the first light of dawn gently kisses the earth, I begin my day with a noble resolution – to be a servant unto others, for in service, I shall find the true essence of leadership.

I shall don the mantle of humility as I move through the day, recognizing that each soul I encounter is endowed with dreams and hopes just as vibrant and worthy as my own. In the echoing silence of my heart, a solemn vow resonates, committing me to uplift, support, and nurture, acting as the gentle wind beneath the wings of those in my charge.

Yes, a servant leader is the visage I shall present to the world. Power and control, though tempting, shall not beguile me into their intoxicating embrace. For true leadership whispers, it does not shout; supports it does not suppress; and it illuminates, never overshadows.

My ears shall be sanctuaries of understanding, always open, ever receptive to the symphonies and soliloquies of those I lead. Their concerns shall not fall on barren ground but shall be seeded within the fertile soil of my consciousness, tended with care and consideration.

With hands extended, not to take, but to give, I shall be a beacon of support and encouragement. In times of triumph, mine shall be the soft clap in the chorus of accolades, gently pushing them to bask in the spotlight they have earned. In times of tribulation, mine shall be the shoulder offered, the silent strength upon which they can lean without fear or hesitation.

Eyes, clear and unclouded by the mist of arrogance, shall see beyond the veil of titles and positions, perceiving the irreplaceable value of each individual. No task shall be deemed too menial, no role insignificant, for in the grand tapestry of success, every thread holds importance, every color contributes to the masterpiece.

With each dawn, I shall be reborn, renewed in my vow to be a servant leader. With a spirit unburdened by the weight of ego, I shall lead by example, living the principles I espouse, embodying the values I champion.

Through the ebb and flow of the day, through the cycle of seasons, in moments of uncertainty and epochs of clarity, this Title shall be my compass, guiding me gently towards the zenith of servant leadership. For in serving, I lead, and in leading, I serve, completing the circle of influence and impact, weaving a legacy of inspiration for generations yet unborn.

So, with the first ray of sunlight casting its glow upon the canvas of the day, I step forth, Title Marked Seven in hand, heart aligned with the timeless principle etched upon its surface: Be a servant leader. And as the sun sets, bathing the sky in hues of gold and crimson, I shall rest, knowing that in service, I have truly led, and in leadership, I have genuinely served.

———◦/◦/◦———

Alfred held onto that last sentence for a little while longer than the rest, allowing it to linger like a deep breath of fresh air.

He felt like he knew this, as if he utterly understood the wisdom behind it. He imagined he'd heard it somewhere before but couldn't quite place it.

And then it struck.

"For true leadership whispers, it does not shout; it supports, does not suppress; and it illuminates, never overshadows."

Jesus. The greatest known leader of all time made a global impact that has lasted thousands of years by serving others.

Matthew 20:28 – "…just as the Son of Man did not come to be served, but to **serve**, and to give His life as a ransom for many."

Luke 22:27 – "I am among you as one who **serves**."

Alfred opened his Bible app and searched for Bible verses that spoke about service to others.

Galatians 5:13 – "You, my brothers, and sisters, were called to be free. But do not use your freedom to indulge in the flesh; rather, **serve** one another humbly in love."

1 Peter 4:10 – "Each of you should use whatever gift you have received to **serve** others, as faithful stewards of God's grace in its various forms."

Again, Alfred sat back in his chair. He would like to say he epitomizes everything he just read, but the truth was, though he aligned with and believed in the principles, his daily actions would say differently.

There were many times where he lost sight of others' desires and was anxiously focused on his own. There were many days where he purposely avoided hard conversations, or certain people who he knew saw the world differently than him.

Alfred had always been a leader who was willing to jump in and help others, but if he were honest, he couldn't really call himself a true "servant-leader." Not by these standards, not even close. Most of his actions were selfish. He helped people when it was convenient for him. He helped people when it benefited him. But he rarely sought out opportunities to serve. He didn't lead with service, he reacted with it.

Alfred now fully understood why Doreen was feeling the way she was feeling. He appreciated her, and even went as far as to tell her such occasionally, but he rarely took the time to actually **serve** her. To make her the most important person in the room. To truly treat her as though she was a not just a part of the team, but a part of the family.

CHAPTER 14
SEEKING OPPORTUNITIES TO SERVE

"Without knowledge, action is useless and knowledge without action is futile."
—Abu Bakr

Alfred knew what he needed to do but wasn't exactly sure how to do it. It would be one thing to say, "Okay, I'm going to be a servant leader now." But he knew that wouldn't work. He needed a system, a process. A way to apply the wisdom from the Titles tangibly, and make it stick.

He recalled listening to a podcast awhile back and had heard someone say, "Show me your calendar, and I will show you your future." Considering the future is what he wanted to change, he decided his calendar would be a suitable place to start.

His current schedule basically was an open slate filled with constant interruptions, and lack of focus. He would go about each day, starting off with a wonderful morning meeting, and then dive into whatever was in front of him at the time. This, Alfred knew, was what had to change.

He started with Monday. The first day of every week, and the most important one for getting momentum going. Mondays were usually a little bit slower as far as incoming customers, but at the same time, pretty busy for his employees following up on the weekend's activities. Alfred decided this would be a wonderful day to meet one-on-one with each of his managers/leaders and create space to make sure they had everything they needed, including any direction from him.

In order to make it work, that would mean no meetings on Mondays with anyone outside of his organization. He would start the daily morning meeting at 8:30, followed by a group manager meeting at 9:00 am. Then at 9:30 he would clean up any quick emails or voicemails from the weekend, and at 10:00 am he would start having the one-on-ones every half an hour until 5:00 P.M. except from noon to one, where he would eat lunch, and again check any urgent emails or voicemails.

During the one-on-ones he would put his phone away, close the door to his office, and make sure everyone knew not to interrupt unless it was an absolute emergency. This time belonged to his leaders, and it was important that he stuck to that for both his ability to stay consistent, and for them to feel special, important, and like they were the only one.

Something that was common at Smith Chevrolet was that vendor reps would come by unannounced as they were making their rounds visiting all their dealer clients. This was something Alfred was going to have to eliminate, so he jumped on his computer, and with a little AI guidance, he put together an email that would be sent out to every company he was doing business with.

Subject: New Meeting Schedule: Office Availability on Tuesdays Only

Dear [Company Name],

I trust this message finds you well. I want to inform you of a change in my office availability for meetings and visits. Starting [Effective Date], I will be scheduling meetings and visits with our business partners exclusively on Tuesdays.

This adjustment in my schedule is designed to streamline my workweek, allowing for more focused and productive interactions with our valued partners. By concentrating meetings on Tuesdays, we aim to enhance the efficiency of our collaboration while ensuring that I can devote ample time to your needs.

Please take note of this change, and kindly reach out to me or my assistant to arrange a meeting on a Tuesday that is convenient for both parties. While I understand that this may require some adjustments on your end, this will ultimately lead to more effective and productive interactions between us.

I appreciate your understanding and cooperation in this matter. I value our business relationship greatly and am committed to maintaining a high level of engagement and service.

Thank you for your attention to this update, and please do not hesitate to reach out if you have any questions or require further clarification. I look forward to continuing our successful partnership in this new meeting schedule.

Warm regards,

[Your Name] [Your Title]

[Your Contact Information]

He then went to his calendar and blocked off 10 A.M. to 4 P.M. on every Tuesday for vendor meetings. They could come during lunch if they'd like, but anything outside of that window was now strictly off limits. No matter what, Alfred was not going to allow other people to dictate his focus on building a great company and being able to best serve his team.

Then came Wednesdays. They would be a perfect day to focus on marketing. Instead of randomly putting together ads whenever the distributors demanded it, Alfred decided he would use most of his time constructing quality marketing campaigns for both their paid, and organic strategies. Wednesday would also be a great day to audit current marketing data, check in on the 8-5-3-1 formula, and manage other aspects regarding the marketing side of the automotive triangle. This would also be a great day to shoot any video footage needed, and to make sure to involve the team in promotions, and social media content.

Thursdays Alfred would focus on the Inventory side of the Automotive Triangle. He would ensure the buyers were doing an excellent job of sourcing inventory, and that pricing was posted and effective. He would also run some quick spot checks to make sure cars were photographed properly and merchandised correctly. All things inventory would take place on Thursdays. This included acquisition, service, sales, and everything in between. The inventory needed to be tight, and this was a great day to attend to that.

Friday was the perfect day to dig into the last side of the triangle, People and Processes. He decided he would start each Friday morning with a daily meeting, followed by a "Contracts in Transit" meeting with his finance managers, and his head of accounting. They would go through every single unfunded deal, or uncollected down payment, work together on a solution, and then act immediately to get the deals across the finish line. Whether that meant calling a customer right there or sending a salesperson out to pick up a bank stipulation, they would handle it.

These meetings would last about an hour and a half and then afterwards Alfred would move over to his Front-Line Sales department. Here he would be in contact with the team, take a few calls, and monitor lead response times and the effectiveness of their responses. He would stay there until noon where he would then choose one or two of his team members to join him for lunch.

After lunch, Alfred set it up to where he would monitor and audit each process they had in place in the dealership. If it had anything to do with transacting with a customer, Alfred looked into it. He monitored everything from getting a copy of a driver's license, to asking for referrals and Google reviews after every purchase. It would be a day where he would be directly involved with the day-to-day activities of the store and could use his time with the team to really seek opportunities to serve.

In the end, Alfred had created a calendar that was filled with an intentional tapestry of works that would allow him to do the work that needed to be done, as well as interact with his team individually, and collectively.

He sat back and looked at what he had created and was rather pleased. Upon further examination though, he realized he'd left out something rather important. The schedule was set up in a way that he could serve, and make people feel special, important, and like they were the only one, but he still didn't feel like other than Friday it left any space for him to seek opportunities to serve. So, Alfred found two, thirty-minute windows on each day of the week and labeled them simply "Seek Opportunities to Serve." Now he would get two reminders each day to get up, get out of his office, and go look for someone to help. Whether it be an employee, a customer, or one of his vendors, Alfred was determined to create space for this particularly important activity.

In the end his calendar looked like this:

SEEKING OPPORTUNITIES TO SERVE

	MON	TUE	WED	THU	FRI
8 AM	Sales Meeting, 8:30am	Sales Meeting, 8:30am	Sales Meeting, 8:30am	Sales Meeting, 8:30am	Sales Meeting, 8:30am
9 AM	Manager Meeting, 9am	Seek Opportunities to Serve, 9am	Seek Opportunities to Serve, 9am	Seek Opportunities to Serve, 9am	Contracts in Transit Meeting 9 – 10:30am
10 AM	Emails and Voicemails, 9:30am	Emails and Voicemails, 9:30am	Emails and Voicemails, 9:30am	Emails and Voicemails, 9:30am	
	Manager One-on-One Meetings 10am – 12pm	Vendor Meetings 10am – 12pm	Marketing Audit 10am – 12pm	Inventory Analysis 10 – 11am	Front Line Sales Visit 10:30am – 12pm
11 AM				Review Buying Plan & Acquisition Performance 11am – 12pm	
12 PM	Lunch, Emails, Voicemails 12 – 1pm	Lunch, Emails, Voicemails 12 – 1pm	Lunch, Emails, Voicemails 12 – 1pm	Lunch, Emails, Voicemails 12 – 1pm	Lunch with Front Lines Sales Rep 12 – 1pm
1 PM	Manager One-on-One Meetings 1 – 5pm	Vendor Meetings 1 – 5pm	B-5-3-1 Analysis / Identify Areas of Opportunity 1 – 2pm	Pricing Audit & Aged Inventory Review 1 – 2pm	Processes Audit 1 – 5pm
2 PM			Campaign Brainstorm & Strategy Development 2 – 3pm	Reconditioning Audit 2 – 3pm	
3 PM			Marketing Video Content Shoot 3 – 5pm	Photos & Merchandising Audit 3 – 4pm	
4 PM				Lot Walk 4 – 5pm	
5 PM	Seek Opportunities to Serve, 5pm	Seek Opportunities to Serve, 5pm	Seek Opportunities to Serve, 5pm	Seek Opportunities to Serve, 5pm	Seek Opportunities to Serve, 5pm
	Emails/Other Pressing Events, 5:30pm	Emails/Other Pressing Events, 5:30pm	Emails/Other Pressing Events, 5:30pm	Emails/Other Pressing Events, 5:30pm	Emails/Other Pressing Events, 5:30pm
6 PM	Finish Items Requiring Attention, 6pm	Finish Items Requiring Attention, 6pm	Finish Items Requiring Attention, 6pm	Finish Items Requiring Attention, 6pm	Finish Items Requiring Attention, 6pm
	Seek Opportunities to Serve, 6:30pm				

Alfred then decided he would start implementing his calendar the very next Monday. He informed his team of their one-on-one time slots, filled in each one on his calendar by name, and looked forward to the new schedule ahead, and when Monday came around, Alfred put things in motion.

At first it was difficult. People struggled to honor the meetings Alfred was having and would interrupt him constantly. Alfred, understanding it would take sixty-seven days before these changes became easier to do than to not do, was patient. He would remind the interrupter that this time slot was held for his team leader, and he would let them know they were empowered to make the best decision in the interest of the company.

This not only made the person in front of him feel important, but it also allowed Alfred to give other members of the team more responsibility and ultimately more ownership in their decisions. It was a win win for all involved.

As the week progressed, vendors continued to try and stop in throughout the weekdays, and each time they were turned away. Many of them complained that they were only in the area on Fridays, or Mondays, but Alfred had directed his receptionist to kindly respond to them with the following. "Alfred is available and willing to sit down with anyone and everyone who is currently doing business with, or looking to start doing business with Smith Chevrolet, on Tuesdays between 10 am and 4 pm. Would you like to schedule an appointment?"

That was it. No other response was acceptable, and no other time would be allotted. If the company wanted to do business with Smith Chevrolet, they would have to figure it out, simple as that.

One of the more startling revelations was when Alfred was "Seeking Opportunities to Serve." An alarm would go off on his phone and he would finish what he was doing. He would then get up and go for a walk.

He would walk around the entire dealership from sales, to service, to detail, parts, and accounting. He would walk around and say hello to everyone he saw and ask if anyone needed any help. The response that he got was "No" 99% of the time.

After doing this for a few weeks Alfred realized that with him being the boss, no one wanted to seem incompetent, so they told him they didn't need help even when they did.

It's hard to tell the boss the truth.

So, Alfred changed his approach. He would walk around greeting his team, and then simply ask, "What are you working on?" This sparked a conversation that at times would open the door to any frustration Alfred's team member may have been facing. He would then use that opportunity to slide in and assist.

Alfred also found that on these walks he would run into a lot of customers. At times, he could tell by the look on their faces that they were angry, upset, frustrated, or some combination of the three. When he came across these situations he would then lean in and say, "Hello, my name is Alfred Smith, and I just want you to know that you've got a friend in the car business." He would shake their hand firmly and give them a small nod, indicating they could trust him. It was amazing how many customers would then share their frustrations with Alfred and open the door to him being able to get involved in serving them.

Alfred continued to stick to the schedule, and in time found himself getting increasingly important work done, while also having a better understanding of the challenges his team was facing. Comradery was increasing, and the team was starting to get this 'Family" feel to it.

The most surprising part though, was Alfred started getting fewer interruptions as time went on. People were getting a clear understanding of his schedule, but even more importantly they were starting to get a clear understanding of **their own** schedule.

Alfred was a bit taken aback at how quickly everyone adapted. The team knew that if there was an issue on a Monday, Alfred would be tied up, and though he trusted them to make decisions, they also knew in the back of their mind that they would either see him during his "Seeking Opportunities to Serve" walk around the dealership daily, or in their next week's one-on-one.

Either way, they stopped bringing everything to Alfred's desk, and instead waited until it was their turn for his undivided attention. It was easy to do because his schedule was so predictable. So, unless their hair was on fire, per say, most people took care of what they needed to take care of, and left Alfred alone. It was a beautiful thing!

The months continued to tick by, and Alfred continued to honor his schedule. In time all of his vendors knew he wouldn't meet on any other day but Tuesday, and the marketing companies knew what to expect on Wednesdays. His leaders looked forward to their one-on-ones on Mondays, and everything around the inventory itself always got managed weekly. The finance department had clean C.I.T. (Contracts in Transit) meetings, and the systems and processes in the dealership continued to evolve and get more efficient.

Doreen and Alfred were finishing their meeting one Monday afternoon and as she was walking out, she turned and looked at Alfred with a look of appreciation and respect. "Thank you, Alfred," she expressed. "And just so you know, I never would've really left."

Alfred smiled. Doreen turned and closed the door behind her.

She always had a way of bringing the best out of Alfred.

CHAPTER 15
WHEN EVERYTHING FALLS APART

"Gratitude can transform common days into thanksgivings, turn routine jobs into joy, and change ordinary opportunities into blessings."
—William Arthur Ward

It had only been a few months since Smith Chevrolet sold 300 cars for the first time, and as a surprise to everyone, including Alfred, in February, a short month, they broke 400!

The team was absolutely on fire! The daily morning meetings were now a company ritual. In fact, the meetings were so consistently impactful, that leaders at other dealerships would ask to visit, just to sit in the morning meetings and experience their energy. Smith Chevrolet had become a topic of conversation across the industry, and everyone wanted to know how this tiny little dealership in the middle of a small town was suddenly selling so many cars.

Alfred had been diligent with his Morning 5 routine and now it was so much easier to follow the process than it was to not follow the process. He literally couldn't imagine starting a day any other way and was now in much better shape physically, as well as mentally. His relationship at home with Betty was going great, and his kids seemed to be thriving.

The 8-5-3-1 formula was firmly in place and the standards had been raised across the dealership. He had brand new salespeople coming into his system selling over twenty cars a month, and seasoned veterans breaking forty, and sometimes even fifty, cars a month!

The culture felt very much like a family, and there had been a handful of promotions that had come along with the increase in sales volume.

Alfred felt like he was definitely on his way to becoming more of a servant leader, and he could honestly say that he had done much better about making sure both his customers and his team felt special, felt important, and like they were the only ones. He had developed a habit of tucking his phone away, and also following the L.E.A.D.D. process in all of his training and conversations.

If he had a call to make with an upset customer, he would now remind himself to Listen Encourage Advise and Develop (L.E.A.D.) before he ever picked up the phone. If he needed to have an important conversation with his wife or his kids, again he would follow the acronym (L.E.A.D.) and Listen Encourage Advise and Develop.

One-on-one meetings, daily morning meetings, calling a prospect, it didn't matter, he learned to follow the L.E.A.D.D. process throughout all his communications.

The red and green daily goal board had become a staple of the dealership, and because they would post it regularly on their social media in celebration, it soon could be found popping up in other dealerships across the country. People were actually mirroring this incredibly simple, and yet effective, tool. It truly had changed the way Smith Chevrolet did business.

Alfred didn't even have to put the board together anymore. Every month his sales managers would pull up the data from last year, add 25%, and track each day with red and green markers. Green days got celebrated; red days dismissed. It was such a simple concept and yet had created a tremendously powerful effect.

Everything was moving right along, except…they had run out of room on the lot to park cars. Also, the once smooth and effective service department was really struggling to keep up with the surge of work required to maintain the now much higher number of sold vehicles every month. Every new vehicle had to be inspected before it could be sold, and every used vehicle reconditioned. Not to mention they also had an influx of new customers needing things like oil changes, tire rotations, brake work, etc.

This wasn't surprising, but it was troublesome, nonetheless. They had grown nearly 400% in roughly three years on the sales side of the business, but the lot size and the service department facilities had remained the same.

This combination of a new increase in volume and an old dealership configuration created a situation where cars were being sold before they were prepped and ready. Add to that, customers were also having above-average wait times to get an oil change and other basic maintenance.

Alfred was getting at least two phone calls a day from unhappy customers and monitoring the company's Google reviews had nearly become a full-time job. The dealership was booming, the energy was electric, the profits were fantastic, but at the same time, Alfred was starting to get really frustrated. All the calls were negatively affecting his attitude towards his team, and he was definitely feeling the pressure of trying to keep everyone happy. He hated to admit it, but if things kept up this way, the whole place was going to burst at the seams.

He went back to the chest:

Title VIII

- CERTIFICATE OF TITLE NUMBER VIII -

CARRY AN ATTITUDE OF GRATITUDE

UPON THE CANVAS OF THIS NEW DAY UNFURLS A TITLE MARKED VIII, BEARING WISDOM BOTH SUBTLE AND ROBUST, GENTLE YET COMMANDING. "CARRY AN ATTITUDE OF GRATITUDE," IT SOFTLY MURMURS, ITS VOICE A GENTLE CARESS AGAINST THE VIBRANT TAPESTRY OF LIFE'S CEASELESS EBB AND FLOW.

COMPREHEND, YOU TIRELESS LABORER IN THE FIELDS OF COMMERCE, THAT WITHIN GRATITUDE RESIDES A MAGIC, POTENT AND PURE, AN UNSEEN YET TRANSFORMATIVE FORCE THAT WEAVES THROUGH THE TAPESTRY OF YOUR DAYS, ILLUMINATING THE MUNDANE, CASTING A SANCTIFYING GLOW UPON THE ORDINARY.

TO HARBOR WITHIN YOUR HEART THE SEED OF GRATITUDE IS TO WITNESS IT BLOOM INTO A FLOWER OF INEFFABLE BEAUTY AND FRAGRANCE, RENDERING THE SOIL OF YOUR TOIL FERTILE AND THE SKIES OF YOUR ENDEAVORS CLEAR AND RADIANT. EACH DEWDROP, EACH RAY OF GOLDEN SUN BECOMES A BLESSING CHERISHED AND COUNTED, A GIFT ACKNOWLEDGED WITH A HEART OVERFLOWING AND EYES THAT SEE BEYOND THE VEIL OF THE TRIVIAL.

APPROACH EACH DAWN WITH A SPIRIT LIGHT AND BUOYANT, UNBURDENED BY THE CHAINS OF DISSATISFACTION OR WANT. FOR IN SEEKING, ACKNOWLEDGE RECEIVING: IN ASPIRING, RECOGNIZE ATTAINMENT. LET NOT THE THIRST FOR MORE WITHER THE WELLSPRING OF THANKFULNESS, FOR WITHIN CONTENTMENT LIES THE ELIXIR OF BOUNDLESS JOY, SUCCESS MEASURED NOT BY WORLDLY GAINS BUT BY THE SCALES OF THE HEART.

SURVEY THE HORIZON OF YOUR LIFE, DILIGENT ONE, AND LET YOUR GAZE FALL UPON THE BOUNTIES THAT ARE YOURS. THE TRUST REPOSED UPON YOUR SHOULDERS, THE RESPECT WOVEN INTO THE VERY FABRIC OF YOUR NAME, THE CAMARADERIE OF THOSE WHO JOURNEY ALONGSIDE YOU THROUGH VALLEYS AND OVER HILLS-EACH IS AN UNPARALLELED TREASURE, A GEM TO BE HELD ALOFT IN THE QUIET SANCTUARY OF A GRATEFUL HEART.

EVEN AS STORM CLOUDS GATHER, CASTING SHADOWS LONG AND DEEP, ALLOW THE BEACON OF GRATITUDE TO PIERCE THROUGH THE GLOOM, ILLUMINATING THE SILVER LININGS, THE PROMISES OF A DAWN YET TO COME. EVERY CHALLENGE, EVERY HURDLE IS BUT A STEPPINGSTONE, A CHAPTER IN THE NARRATIVE OF YOUR LEGEND, PENNED WITH INK DIPPED IN THE WELL OF PERSEVERANCE AND GRATITUDE.

THROUGH THE BUSTLING MARKET'S CORRIDORS, AMID THE CALLS OF BUYERS AND SELLERS, LET YOUR STEP BE LIGHT, YOUR SMILE UNBURDENED. CARRY NOT ONLY THE WARES OF TRADE IN YOUR HANDS BUT ALSO THE INVISIBLE, INTANGIBLE GIFT OF GRATITUDE, OFFERING IT GENEROUSLY, SPREADING ITS FRAGRANCE LIKE THE GENTLE BREEZE THAT WAFTS THROUGH ORCHARDS, CARRYING THE SCENT OF RIPE FRUIT AND BLOOMING FLOWERS.

"CARRY AN ATTITUDE OF GRATITUDE," THE TITLE MARKED VIII BECKONS, AND AS YOU HEED ITS CALL, BEHOLD THE TRANSFORMATION UPON THE CANVAS OF YOUR LIFE. COLORS BECOME MORE VIBRANT, SOUNDS MORE HARMONIOUS, AND THE TAPESTRY OF YOUR DAYS WEAVES PATTERNS OF JOY, SUCCESS, AND FULFILLMENT-SPLENDIDLY, UNIQUELY YOURS, AND UNIMAGINED.

The Title Marked VIII

Carry an Attitude of Gratitude

Upon the canvas of this new day unfurls a Title Marked VIII, bearing wisdom both subtle and robust, gentle yet commanding. "Carry An Attitude of Gratitude," it softly murmurs, its voice a gentle caress against the vibrant tapestry of life's ceaseless ebb and flow.

I comprehend, as a tireless laborer in the fields of commerce, that within gratitude resides a magic, potent and pure, an unseen yet transformative force that weaves through the tapestry of my days, illuminating the mundane, casting a sanctifying glow upon the ordinary.

To harbor within my heart the seed of gratitude is to witness it bloom into a flower of ineffable beauty and fragrance, rendering the soil fertile and the skies of my endeavors clear and radiant. Each dewdrop, each ray of golden sun becomes a blessing cherished and counted, a gift acknowledged with a heart overflowing and eyes that see beyond the veil of the trivial.

I will approach each dawn with a spirit light and buoyant, unburdened by the chains of dissatisfaction or want. For in seeking, acknowledge receiving; in aspiring, recognize attainment. Let not the thirst for more wither the wellspring of thankfulness, for within contentment lies the elixir of boundless joy, success measured not by worldly gains but by the scales of the heart.

I will survey the horizon of my life, diligent one, and let my gaze fall upon the bounties that are mine. The trust reposed upon my shoulders, the respect woven into the very fabric of my name, the camaraderie of those who journey alongside me through valleys and over hills—each is an unparalleled treasure, a gem to be held aloft in the quiet sanctuary of a grateful heart.

Even as storm clouds gather, casting shadows long and deep, I will allow the beacon of gratitude to pierce through the gloom, illuminating the silver linings, the promises of a dawn yet to come. Every challenge, every hurdle is but a steppingstone, a chapter in the narrative of my legend, penned with ink dipped in the well of perseverance and gratitude.

Through the bustling market's corridors, amid the calls of buyers and sellers, my step will be light, my smile unburdened. I will carry not only the wares of trade in my hands but also the invisible, intangible gift of gratitude, offering it generously, spreading its fragrance like the gentle breeze that wafts through orchards, carrying the scent of ripe fruit and blooming flowers.

"Carry An Attitude of Gratitude," the Title Marked VIII beckons, and as I heed its call, behold the transformation upon the canvas of my life. Colors become more vibrant, sounds more harmonious, and the tapestry of my days weaves patterns of joy, success, and fulfillment—splendidly, uniquely mine, and unimagined.

Alfred let this one wash over him. He had always felt he was the grateful type and understood the power behind it. Admittedly though, he didn't always display that gratitude and he definitely had moments where he'd lost sight of the blessings in his life. Especially in this current season of upset customers, and a backed-up service department.

He breathed deeply and pondered on how the Titles always seemed to speak exactly to what he was experiencing in the moment.

"Every challenge, every hurdle is but a steppingstone, a chapter in the narrative of your legend, penned with ink dipped in the well of perseverance and gratitude."

Alfred re-read that sentence over and over. He loved how it said *every* hurdle, not *some* hurdles, not *a lot* of hurdles, no, *every* hurdle was a chapter in Alfred's narrative to become a legend. A legend is indeed what Alfred did want to become.

He strived to be the one who carried the legacy that his grandfather started all those years ago proudly. He wanted to make an impact on so many people's lives, that his name would go down in history. He wanted to serve his community, lead his family, and truly live in a way that made a difference.

Alfred wanted all the time invested, all the sacrifices made, all the arduous work, to matter.

Now here he was, up against the ropes, facing unheard of growth and success, and he found himself frustrated, and feeling like the whole thing was going to crumble at any moment.

"Stop it, Alfred," he told himself. "You can do this."

As the Title lay on the desk beside him, Alfred grabbed a notebook and started writing everything he had to be grateful for in the dealership. He wrote down things like his team, his current facility, electricity, and Wi-Fi.

He wrote down the growth they had experienced, the money they'd made, the jobs they'd created. He wrote down everything from computers, to copy machines, to the phone systems, and the CRM. He wrote down tables, chairs, water faucets, and working toilets. He wrote down alarm systems, night lights, and the daily sounds of laughter and success. He wrote down memories, conversations, memorable moments, and the challenges they had overcome. He wrote down speakers, music, videos they had made, and team pictures. He wrote down new systems and processes, new people and of course the Titles themselves. He continued to write and write, and write until he had listed over a hundred items he was grateful for, just within the dealership itself.

When he was done, he took a few minutes and wrote down the obstacles they had in front of them. There were only two. The lot was a bit too small for where they wanted to go, and the service department was backed up from all the growth.

Over a hundred items to be grateful for. Two challenges to overcome. How conniving is the mind that allows us to inflate the negatives amid so much good.

Alfred could solve these things. It would take time, but time is what they had created. The success of the dealership had bought them the luxury of doing things the right way. Before, when they were operating month-to-month, they were always worried about the next monthly statement. Now, Alfred and his team had created a cushion of both cash reserves and cashflow that would allow them to take their time and do things right.

It reminded Alfred of the time he was at an automotive event and Glenn Lundy was on stage telling the story of the *three little pigs*. Glenn told it in a way that was fun and entertaining, and ultimately helped the audience learn a lesson that most people had missed from the original fairy tale.

Alfred went to YouTube, pulled up Glenn Lundy's speech from that event, and sat back to watch it again.

"So, there were these three little pigs, right? They were brothers, and they heard that there was a big bad wolf coming." Glenn Lundy's voice came through the computer speakers "They decided they needed to build some sort of shelter to protect them. None of them really knew anything about building a house of course, and so they each set out to build one their own way."

Glenn continued "Now the first pig had a party to go to that night, so he decided he didn't want to take too much time, and he threw something together quickly. When all was said and done, he had a house made out of hay. Considering the job done, he went wee wee wee all the way to the party." The audience chuckled.

Glenn paused to let the chuckles quiet down, and then jumped right back into the story.

"Now the second little pig saw what his brother had built and was like…'nah…that ain't gonna work.' So, he went and chopped down a couple of trees, took a little more time, and built a fairly decent house made out of wood. It was taking him quite a bit longer than his brother, and the whole time he was thinking about all the fun his brother was having at the party, so in the end, he kind of hurried it up, took a couple shortcuts, slapped it together, and then headed to the party to shake his little pigtail for the rest of the night."

Again, the audience laughed, and Glenn waited. Once the rumble ceased, he moved forward.

"The third brother saw the house made out of hay, and the other made out of wood, and was like…'Nope, this ain't gonna work.' He then went on YouTube and started doing research on building a house. It seemed like bricks were the way to go, so he started looking up how to lay bricks. After watching a few dozen videos, he went to Lowes, bought all the supplies he needed, brought them all back to the forest, and painstakingly started laying bricks one by one. It took a lot of time to lay each one perfectly connected to the last, but after a lot of work, he finally had built a house. He missed the party, he missed the fun, he missed all the things his brothers got to participate in, but in the end, he had made a brick house to be proud of."

"Now here comes the big, bad, wolf, and he goes up to the house made from straw, knocks on the door, and says…'Little pig, little pig, let me in! The pig says…" At this point, Glenn gestures to the audience and in unison they all shout 'Not by the hair of my chinny chin chin!"

There's a huge roar of laughter. Glenn can't help but laugh with them this time.

"Then the wolf says, 'Then I will huff, and I'll puff, and I will blow your house in!' and he does! And the little pig goes running! Then the big bad wolf goes to the house made from wood and knocks on the door…"

At this point Glenn continues to work the crowd. Everyone is chanting the lines from the nursery rhyme and of course laughing in the process. After the wolf gets to the house made from brick, Glenn finishes with a twist. The twist was what had really stuck with Alfred and caused him to remember the talk again at this very moment.

"….and he huffs, and he puffs, and he CAN'T blow the house down. So, what does he end up doing? He goes away, and the brick house is left standing, and the little pig is safe.

'But here is the part of the book that most people miss.' At this point Glenn draws the audience in with a well-placed pause. There is not a sound in the room, you could literally hear a pin drop.

"The part that everyone missed is that on the second to the last page of the book it shows the big bad wolf walking away defeated, and guess who is in the house? Not just the one brother who built the house, but actually all three pigs. You see, because the one brother took the time to learn how to pour cement, and to lay the bricks. Because the one little pig was willing to sacrifice the parties and messing around with his friends. Because the one pig was willing to take the time to craft a home that he could be proud of, one that would stand the test of time. Because of that, he not only created a safe place for himself, but a safe place for his brothers who were not willing to make that sacrifice."

Glenn continued in a low, deep, soft tone:

"You all have people in your life who you love. People that are going to refuse to do the work. You, however, can choose to do the work that it takes to build a solid foundation, and protect yourself and those you love against the big bad wolves of life. Listen, we all know the storms are coming. They're gonna huff, and puff, and try to blow your house down!

"So do the work, and make sure you don't end up being somebody else's porkchop."

Alfred chuckled. Glenn's talks always did have a way to lift his spirits. Even if he was using some old fairy tale to do so.

Due to the application of the Titles, Alfred had put Smith Chevrolet in a position where they could take the time to do things the right way. He had built a solid foundation and was going to continue to do so. They had their struggles to overcome, but all Alfred needed to do was take lessons from the *Three Little Pigs* story, continue to mix cement, and lay those bricks. In the end they would have a safe place where everyone could thrive, and Alfred's legacy would continue to expand.

Remaining grateful for the work they had done, and the opportunity they had ahead was more important now than ever, too many people's lives were at stake.

With a little research, some ingenuity, and intentional focus on a solution, he would find a way to be able to store and service all the vehicles necessary for growth. There was no need to panic, and no party he needed to run off to, he just needed to keep laying bricks, one perfectly laid brick at a time.

CHAPTER 16
CHAMPIONS ATTRACTING CHAMPIONS

> *"Character may be manifested*
> *in the great moments,*
> *but it is made in the small ones."*
> **—Phillips Brooks**

It was a warm Tuesday in the spring and Alfred was sitting in an interview across from yet another long-time car veteran. The applicant was telling him a story about how he had been in the business for 20 years, and of course every dealership he had worked at before, he had been the best one there.

This wasn't a new situation. It seemed like every time Alfred had an interview with someone who had automotive experience, they were either the top salesperson, or the sales manager that made all the difference, or the finance guy that put up the best numbers, or the GM that brought the store from obscurity to number one in their zone, their region, the country, or the world!

These conversations were always so tiresome. Alfred would ask a simple question, "If you were the best, why did they let you go?" And of course, that would always be answered by some sort of excuse about how the owners didn't care about them, they got treated poorly, or something changed that they didn't agree with, so they had to get out of there. It was always a story about how the candidate in front of Alfred was the victim, and the place they had either quit or gotten fired from was the bad guy.

This was the story…every single time.

Now because they had been growing so fast, they were always in need of new people. The promotions always came from inside, but entry level roles were constantly needing to be filled. At this point interviewing and hiring people was just about a full-time job. Seemingly every day, someone would come by asking to fill out an application, and to get in front of "the owner" or "a manager" to discuss how great they were.

Alfred felt like there had to be a better way, so he went and grabbed the chest.

Title IX

- CERTIFICATE OF TITLE NUMBER IX -

HIRE AND FIRE ON CHARACTER NOT CREDENTIALS

IN THE HALLOWED CORRIDORS OF ANCIENT WISDOM AND WHISPERED TRUTHS, OPEN YOURSELF TO THE TITLE MARKED IX, WHICH BEARS INSIGHTS STEEPED IN THE TIMELESS ESSENCE OF CHARACTER-A GUIDING LIGHT FOR INTEGRITY AND STEADFASTNESS.

LISTEN, DILIGENT SEEKER OF EXCELLENCE, TO THIS SILENT YET POWERFUL AXIOM: HIRE NOT SOLELY BY GILDED QUALIFICATIONS OR THE TRIUMPHANT FANFARE OF ACADEMIA, BUT BY THE UNYIELDING AND INCORRUPTIBLE SUBSTANCE OF CHARACTER.

IN THE REALMS OF COMMERCE AND THE SACRED HALLS OF BUSINESS, THE PARCHMENT OF CREDENTIALS MAY GLITTER WITH ALLURE, BUT IT IS THE CORE AND MARROW OF A PERSON'S CHARACTER THAT WILL ENDURE THROUGH STORMS AND NAVIGATE MURKY WATERS OF CHALLENGE AND CHANGE.

EMBARK, THEREFORE, ON YOUR QUEST WITH EYES THAT PERCEIVE BEYOND THE SURFACE, DISCERNING THE INVISIBLE FRAMEWORK OF VALUES AND ETHICS-THE SILENT COMPASS THAT GUIDES THROUGH NIGHT AND DAWN, TEMPEST, AND TRANQUILITY.

GATHER AROUND YOU INDIVIDUALS OF STERLING CHARACTER, FOR THEY WILL STAND UNWAVERING WHEN SKIES DARKEN AND THE GROUND TREMBLES. THEIR LOYALTY WILL NOT SWAY FOR GOLDEN OFFERS, AND THEIR INTEGRITY WILL NOT CRUMBLE UNDER THE WEIGHT OF TEMPTATION.

CONSIDER, WITH DUE REFLECTION, THAT CHARACTER IS THE INVISIBLE ARCHITECT CRAFTING EDIFICES OF TRUST AND FORTRESSES OF RELIABILITY. IT IS THE SILENT PROMISE WHISPERED THROUGH ACTIONS, A COMMITMENT PAINTED NOT IN WORDS BUT IN DEEDS-UNDYING AND UNYIELDING.

WHEN YOUR SANCTUARY OF PRODUCTS REQUIRES STEWARDS AND GUARDIANS, SEEK NOT ONLY THOSE ARMED WITH DEGREES AND ACCOLADES. LOOK INSTEAD FOR THOSE IN WHOSE HEARTS RESIDE THE PRINCIPLES OF HONESTY, DILIGENCE, AND SERVICE, FOR THEY SHALL BE THE TRUE CUSTODIANS OF YOUR LEGACY AND THE HONORABLE STANDARD-BEARERS OF YOUR BRAND.

ENTRUST THEM WITH THE RESPONSIBILITY OF SHEPHERDING YOUR PRECIOUS METALLIC STEEDS. LET THEM BE THE FACE AND VOICE OF YOUR ENTERPRISE, FOR IN THEIR HANDS, THE INVISIBLE BANNER OF CHARACTER SHALL FLUTTER, CASTING ITS PROTECTIVE AND MAGNETIC AURA. IT WILL ATTRACT SOULS OF SIMILAR DISPOSITION AND KINDLE THE FLAME OF LOYALTY AMONG THOSE WHO ENGAGE WITH ITS ENERGY.

REMEMBER, WHEN THE INK OF CREDENTIALS FADES AND THE PAPER OF QUALIFICATIONS YELLOWS WITH AGE, IT IS CHARACTER, ETERNAL AND UNBLEMISHED, THAT WILL CONTINUE TO SHINE-A LIGHTHOUSE GUIDING YOUR SHIP THROUGH ALTERNATING CURRENTS OF CALM AND STORM, SUCCESS, AND CHALLENGE.

LET THIS TITLE BE YOUR REMINDER AND GUIDE, SILENTLY ECHOING IN THE CORRIDORS OF YOUR CONSCIOUSNESS, URGING YOU TO VALUE CHARACTER ABOVE CREDENTIALS. IT IS THE TRUE MEASURE AND PREDICTOR OF SUCCESS, BOTH IN THE TEMPORAL REALM OF COMMERCE AND THE ETERNAL DIMENSION OF LEGACY AND HONOR.

WITH THIS WISDOM ETCHED UPON YOUR HEART AND MIND, VENTURE FORTH WITH CONFIDENCE AND DISCERNMENT, ASSEMBLING AROUND YOU A SQUAD OF INDIVIDUALS WHOSE CHARACTER SHALL BE THE BEDROCK UPON WHICH YOUR EMPIRE OF SERVICE, EXCELLENCE, AND LEGACY SHALL ETERNALLY STAND.

The Title Marked IX

Hire and Fire on Character, Not Credentials

In the hallowed corridors of ancient wisdom and whispered truths, open yourself to the Title Marked IX, which bears insights steeped in the timeless essence of character—a guiding light for integrity and steadfastness.

Listen, diligent seeker of excellence, to this silent yet powerful axiom: Hire not solely by gilded qualifications or the triumphant fanfare of academia, but by the unyielding and incorruptible substance of character.

In the realms of commerce and the sacred halls of business, the parchment of credentials may glitter with allure, but it is the core and marrow of a person's character that will endure through storms and navigate murky waters of challenge and change.

Embark, therefore, on a quest with eyes that perceive beyond the surface, discerning the invisible framework of values and ethics—the silent compass that guides through night and dawn, tempest, and tranquility.

Gather around you individuals of sterling character, for they will stand unwavering when skies darken and the ground trembles. Their loyalty will not sway for golden offers, and their integrity will not crumble under the weight of temptation.

Consider, with due reflection, that character is the invisible architect crafting edifices of trust and fortresses of reliability. It is the silent promise whispered through actions, a commitment painted not in words but in deeds—undying and unyielding.

When your sanctuary of products requires stewards and guardians, seek not only those armed with degrees and accolades. Look instead for those in whose hearts reside the principles of honesty, diligence, and service, for they shall be the true custodians of your legacy and the honorable standard-bearers of your brand.

Entrust them with the responsibility of shepherding your precious metallic steeds. Let them be the face and voice of your enterprise, for in their hands, the invisible banner of character shall flutter, casting its protective and magnetic aura. It will attract souls of similar disposition and kindle the flame of loyalty among those who engage with its energy.

Remember, when the ink of credentials fades and the paper of qualifications yellows with age, it is character, eternal and unblemished, that will continue to shine—a lighthouse guiding your ship through alternating currents of calm and storm, success, and challenge.

Let this Title be your reminder and guide, silently echoing in the corridors of your consciousness, urging you to value character above credentials. It is the true measure and predictor of success, both in the temporal realm of commerce and the eternal dimension of legacy and honor.

With this wisdom etched upon your heart and mind, venture forth with confidence and discernment, assembling around you a squad of individuals whose character shall be the bedrock upon which your empire of service, excellence, and legacy shall eternally stand.

It was an interesting Title. Alfred began to think about how they had always done things at the store. He could even recall ads he had written for hiring campaigns, and conversations he'd had around searching for EXPERIENCED salespeople, or EXPERIENCED technicians, or any other position for that matter. They were always looking for people with experience.

But if he really thought back through history, he was reminded that some of his best employees of all time started with zero, or little experience.

There was Savanna, who started in the detail department cleaning cars, made her way to sales, then became a finance manager and is now one of his highest producing team members.

Meredith, who had been a hairdresser in a previous life and was now their top salesperson selling over forty cars a month. (Sometimes fifty!)

Of course, Leslie, the server from the Jerry's restaurant down the street, that got hired as a receptionist and then insisted on getting a log-in for sales training. She made her way to sales, became a top salesperson and then after a promotion to the finance department, absolutely dominated that space.

And Michael, he was also a server at the local Jerry's restaurant. He came in as a salesperson, became a finance manager, became a sales manager, and something unlocked in him, and he started developing all kinds of digital tools that completely changed the way the sales team did business and communicated with one another.

Jerry, the football player, went from sales to sales manager, and now General Sales Manager.

Sahar the butcher; Oaklynn the ADT security installer; Robin the warehouse manager at the Scentsy factory; Laura the athletic gym director; Everett the bartender, Caroline the Army veteran; Robert the construction worker; James the furniture salesman; the list went on and on of people who started at Smith Chevrolet either on the sales side, or on the service side, with absolutely no experience, and became pillars of the dealership's success.

Alfred was a bit taken aback. How had he not seen this before? He was looking for experienced people, hiring people who had either quit or got fired somewhere else, and wondering why it always felt like he couldn't find any good people.

Of course, the pool of candidates was small if experience were required, but how many people could potentially come to work for him if he simply focused on people's character and threw experience out the window?

He decided to change things up. He sat and wrote down all his current hiring issues on one side of a piece of paper. Then he made a conscious commitment to do the opposite of those things, and he put what he would like to do on the right side of the paper.

It ended up looking like this:

Always hiring	Only hiring quarterly
Experience required	If more than two years of experience, not hirable
New hires just get thrown into the mix	New hires will go through a group training and onboarding process
Background check disqualifies candidate	Background check helps tell the story of the candidate. We hire on character, not credentials
Applicants always popping in	Only accepting applications for two weeks prior to onboarding
A lot of applicants are not willing to do some of the things we do with video and social media	Applicant must submit 90-second video in order to gain an actual in person interview
Leadership applicants do not understand our culture	All new hires must start at the lowest level of that department
Do not know who we are really hiring, everyone has a good interview	Personality tests will be part of the hiring process, and an avatar of exactly who we are looking for must be in place

Alfred was amazed. As he read the list again, making sure he wasn't missing anything, he realized how counter-intuitive all of this was to not only how he had been doing business, but ultimately how the entire auto industry had been doing business.

No one had a good new hire process!

No one controlled when and how they hired!

No one was seeking inexperienced people and refusing to hire experienced ones!

"An avatar? Shut up! This is good stuff!" Alfred said aloud to himself.

Alfred was pleased. He glanced over at the mirror hanging in his office and was a bit surprised at who he saw looking back. The man he was three years ago was gone. He had completely disappeared thanks to 'The Morning 5" and all of the other Titles he had been able to implement in the dealership. This new Alfred was unrecognizable, not just physically, but in thought and in words.

Not to mention all the extra money he was making…that was pretty cool too.

Alfred went to work putting a new hiring process in place. He decided they would hire in groups and bring in their first group the first week of June. Then going forward, every three months they would bring in more people, accepting applications only in the two weeks prior to the onboarding class. They would also take a full two weeks to on-board people, making sure they knew everything they needed to know to be successful, and also ensuring clarity for the new hire of what to expect. He started by grabbing a year-at-a-glance calendar and filled it out with what the hiring schedule would look like:

200%
ELITE AUTOMOTIVE CLUB

JANUARY	FEBRUARY	MARCH
Su Mo Tu We Th Fr Sa	Su Mo Tu We Th Fr Sa	Su Mo Tu We Th Fr Sa
1 2 3 4 5 6	1 2 3	1 2
7 8 9 10 11 12 13	4 5 6 7 8 9 10	3 4 5 6 7 8 9
14 15 16 17 18 19 20	11 12 13 14 15 16 17	10 11 12 13 14 15 16
21 22 23 24 25 26 27	18 19 20 21 22 23 24	17 18 **APPLICATION** 23
28 29 30 31	25 26 27 28 29	24 25 26 27 28 29 30
		31

APRIL	MAY	JUNE
Su Mo Tu We Th Fr Sa	Su Mo Tu We Th Fr Sa	Su Mo Tu We Th Fr Sa
1 **ONBOARDING** 6	1 2 3 4	1
7 8 9 10 11 12 13	5 6 7 8 9 10 11	2 3 4 5 6 7 8
14 15 16 17 18 19 20	12 13 14 15 16 17 18	9 10 11 12 13 14 15
21 22 23 24 25 26 27	19 20 21 22 23 24 25	16 17 **APPLICATION** 22
28 29 30	26 27 28 29 30 31	23 24 25 26 27 28 29
		30

JULY	AUGUST	SEPTEMBER
Su Mo Tu We Th Fr Sa	Su Mo Tu We Th Fr Sa	Su Mo Tu We Th Fr Sa
1 **ONBOARDING** 6	1 2 3	1 2 3 4 5 6 7
7 8 9 10 11 12 13	4 5 6 7 8 9 10	8 9 10 11 12 13 14
14 15 16 17 18 19 20	11 12 13 14 15 16 17	15 16 **APPLICATION** 21
21 22 23 24 25 26 27	18 19 20 21 22 23 24	22 23 24 25 26 27 28
28 29 30 31	25 26 27 28 29 30 31	29 30

OCTOBER	NOVEMBER	DECEMBER
Su Mo Tu We Th Fr Sa	Su Mo Tu We Th Fr Sa	Su Mo Tu We Th Fr Sa
ONBOARDING 5	1 2	1 2 3 4 5 6 7
6 7 8 9 10 11 12	3 4 5 6 7 8 9	8 9 10 11 12 13 14
13 14 15 16 17 18 19	10 11 12 13 14 15 16	15 16 **APPLICATION** 21
20 21 22 23 24 25 26	17 18 19 20 21 22 23	22 23 24 25 26 27 28
27 28 29 30 31	24 25 26 27 28 29 30	29 30 31

Once all of that was put together, Alfred took some time and thought through what a full schedule for on-boarding should look like. There were a lot of caveats to the business that people needed to know early, and he wanted to make sure it was both a thorough process, and an efficient one.

He decided the best way to do it was to empower his leaders to run the on-boarding in two-hour segments, with him supplementing it at times, so that all together it would be a family affair.

Each of his leaders could teach the thing they were an expert at. Sales could teach sales. The CFO could teach the pay plan and accounting aspects. Human resources could teach about benefits, vacation pay, things like that. **Each aspect of onboarding would be taught to the new hires directly by the leaders in the organization who Alfred had hand-selected because they were the absolute best.**

While building the schedule out, he realized that the on boarding would actually be more like a boot camp. They could actually hire people with an understanding that it was just a two-week contract. Then they could put them through their paces for two weeks, have them work open to close every day, and at the end of the two weeks, IF they made it through, they then would become full-time employees.

This would allow Alfred and the team to really get to know someone when they are at their worst. They would be tired from long days, frustrated from having to learn so much in a short amount of time, and adjusting to a new culture. All of these things would create stress on the applicant, allowing Alfred to see what they were really made of.

He loved the idea, so he ran with it, building a two-week on-boarding schedule that would be packed with all the things the new hire would need to know, assuming they were brand new to the business. They would search for people with zero experience, and place zero expectations on them, other than that they had to be hard workers, with good character. This would also allow his team to get a better idea of who they were dealing with.

When he was nearing the end of his brainstorming, he decided the best thing would be for the new hires to start on Monday by joining the rest of the team in their daily morning meeting. Then every hour after would be filled with things like getting logins and passwords for the computers, key machines, and CRM's, meeting with Human Resources to understand their 401k and benefits, going over the history of the company, showing them highlight videos and fun ad campaigns, giving them a tour of the facility and introducing them to people; things like that.

Then at 5:00 p.m. they would move from the classroom style training to on-the-floor training, where they would be paired up with some of the top performers in the dealership and instructed to shadow them the rest of the night.

This would allow them to witness things firsthand, in real time, and allow the top-performers to strut a bit and show off their stuff. It was another win-win scenario.

Tuesday would start the same with the daily morning meeting but then the new hires would begin to dive into things more specific to their actual day-to-day work. They would go over all the systems and processes they would need to learn and train on, each in two-hour increments.

In between each two-hour session, Alfred would have some of the other team members come by and share stories of their experience at Smith Chevrolet. They would share how they started from nothing and now were crushing it, or how they never had experience before and now they love it. All the motivational, and inspirational stories that the dealership had created over the years would be brought to the table.

This, he hoped, would inspire the potential new hires, and also allow them to connect to more members of the team. Instead of just being trained by one person, or a handful of people, they would be getting poured into by a diverse group of individuals. From young, old, black, white, male, female, and every other dynamic you can think of, this process would allow each of the candidates to see themselves on the other side of, success, and Alfred believed that would turn out to be one of the most powerful and important pieces of the on-boarding.

Everyone was to have a training session. From the finance managers who would teach about what it means to contract deals and sell products, to the service manager who would explain how the fixed operations side of the business worked. The head of detail would have a session, and of course accounting, sales management, front-line sales reps, marketing; every single department would be represented and asked to teach what they do, and why it is important to the success of the dealership.

Setting up things this way would also make the on-boarding process much more manageable. Instead of a heavy load, it would become a thing where every three months, each leader would have two to four hours that they would need to pour into the new class. Outside of that, they had months where they never had to even worry about it.

Alfred continued to map out Wednesday, Thursday, Friday, and Saturday. He even decided that people should spend a little time working in other departments to be able to understand them better, so on the first Wednesday of the two-week boot camp all new hires were required to spend the day in the detail department washing cars.

Then on the second Wednesday of the camp, they were required to spend time in the service department, checking in customers, and helping write tickets. This gave them a well-rounded respect for other areas of the dealership in which they wouldn't typically spend time. Alfred was hesitant to admit it but it was GENIUS.

At the end of the two weeks, they would have a full understanding of all the workings of the dealership, and also Alfred would have a full understanding of them. If they refused to wash cars because it was "beneath" them, it was easy; he would let them go. If they did not want to get their hands dirty in service, it was a quick exit for the candidate. Couldn't handle the long hours? Drama while in class? No patience, or not wanting to complete all of the training? Couldn't figure out the computers? Wouldn't join in on the social media training?

Refused to cooperate with making videos? Anything like that, and Alfred would just make it easy and say:

"We think we'd be holding you back by allowing you to work here. It appears you might be a better fit somewhere else. Thank you for applying." And on that note, he would turn and walk away.

It was beautiful on paper, and once they started to implement, it was even more beautiful in action. The next hiring quarter, everyone knew what to do and while they were training Alfred would walk by, open the door to the classroom, jump in really quickly to add some additional energy to the room, and then walk out smiling.

They were literally building champions. Instead of trying to hire people with experience and convert them to their ways, they were taking people who didn't know anything different and teaching them things like the 8-5-3-1 formula, The Morning 5, The Four Ps, and so much more.

The ones that made it through the bootcamp would hit the ground running. They were fully equipped to do the job, and to do the job well. As a bonus, they already knew just about every one of their co-workers in the organization. At the very least, they knew all of the leaders, and where to turn if they needed help in any aspect.

All of that was just gravy because in between hiring boot camps … Alfred could only describe it as pure, sweet bliss. The team could focus on doing their job daily, and developing the new people along the way, versus constantly having to interview, train, hire, and fire year-round. It also made a tremendous difference in their ability to recruit, retain, and equip people for success. Hiring on character, not credentials, had introduced Smith Chevrolet to a whole new pool of potential candidates, and brought them into a world of opportunity they never even knew existed.

Once again, a structured, intentional process was changing the game.

After a few quarters of training and making a few tweaks, Alfred ended up putting together a calendar and workbook for the team to use in future classes, and for the first time in company history, Smith Chevrolet had a bonafide hiring and on boarding process that would become the foundation of all they would continue to build on in the future.

WEEK 1	MON	TUES	WED	THURS	FRI	SAT
8:30 - 9:00	MEETING	MEETING	MEETING	MEETING	MEETING	MEETING
9:00 - 11:00	TOUR & HISTORY	EXPECTATIONS	DETAIL ALL DAY	BDM LEAD HANDLING	UNSOLD FOLLOW UP	SHADOW ALL DAY
11:00 - 1:00	LOGINS PURPOSE OF THE TOOLS	NEW / CPO / USED / AS-IS INVENTORY & ACQUISITION	DETAIL ALL DAY	SALES PROCESS ATTITUDE GREETING FACT FINDING APPRAISAL	SOLD FOLLOW UP REPEATS AND REFERRALS	SHADOW ALL DAY
1:00 - 2:00	LUNCH	LUNCH	LUNCH	LUNCH	LUNCH	LUNCH
2:00 - 4:00	CFO PAY PLAN, BENEFITS, ACCOUNTING & OFFICE	RECON PROCESS AND DETAIL	DETAIL ALL DAY	SALES PROCESS SELECTION DEMO TRIAL CLOSE SERVICE WALK	FINANCE WHAT F&I DOES	SHADOW ALL DAY
4:00 - 6:00	HR BENEFITS, EMPLOYEE HANDBOOK	MARKETING ACQUIRING THE OPPORTUNITIES	DETAIL ALL DAY	SALES PROCESS WRITE UP NEGOTIATIONS CLOSE DELIVERY FOLLOW UP	SERVICE MGR FIXED OPS	SHADOW ALL DAY
6:00 - CLOSE	SHADOW	SHADOW	SHADOW	SHADOW	SHADOW	SHADOW ALL DAY

WEEK 2	MON	TUES	WED	THURS	FRI	SAT
8:30 - 9:00	MEETING	MEETING	MEETING	MEETING	MEETING	MEETING
9:00 - 11:00	CRM TRAINING	IMPORTANT VOCABULARY	SERVICE ALL DAY	WARRANTIES FROM MANUFACTURER	HISTORY OF THE BRAND	SHADOW ALL DAY
11:00 - 1:00	WHY BUYS	TRADE WALK	SERVICE ALL DAY	PAPERWORK TITLE & REG	CARS & SMALL SUVS	SHADOW ALL DAY
1:00 - 2:00	LUNCH	LUNCH	LUNCH	LUNCH	LUNCH	LUNCH
2:00 - 4:00	FINANCE BASICS TERM, LTV STD VS SUBVENT PROPER T.O. TO F&I	CLOSING	SERVICE ALL DAY	PROCESSES AND POLICIES	LARGE SUVS & TRUCKS	SHADOW ALL DAY
4:00 - 6:00	CUSTOM FINANCE CREDIT, ABILITY, STABILITY, STRUCTURE, STIPS, FUNDING	LEASING	SERVICE ALL DAY	THE LOT	CSI, REVIEWS, TOOLS FROM MANUFACTURER	SHADOW ALL DAY
6:00 - CLOSE	SHADOW	SHADOW	SHADOW	SHADOW	SHADOW	SHADOW ALL DAY

CHAPTER 17
BOOKS, BOOKS, AND MORE BOOKS

"The more that you read,
the more things you will know.
The more that you learn,
the more places you'll go."
—Dr. Seuss

Five hundred cars. Alfred couldn't believe it. They sold five hundred cars in twenty-six business days. Open Monday through Saturday. Closed on Sunday and including a record Saturday where they sold sixty-three cars in literally twelve hours. They started at 8:30 A.M. that day and went home at 8:30 P.M. Twelve hours. They sold sixty-three cars in twelve hours!

Alfred was elated. This was more than he had ever anticipated they could achieve, and yet oddly enough, he still believed there was so much more there. He was grateful for their success, but definitely not satisfied. He could see it in the data. They were converting leads at 15%, but every time he went in to do an audit, he found mistakes that could've easily increased those conversions.

He now had a team of salespeople all selling at least twenty cars a month, but he still found it curious that he had others selling twice that? Didn't that mean the ones selling twenty cars could maybe sell twenty-five? Or thirty?

And what about marketing? It was in place, and doing well, and yet there were always tweaks that could be made to help it drive more traffic. The team was doing great at posting on social media, but of course they could always do better it seemed.

Service was cranking, as they had just bought four acres around the property, built an additional service building, added fourteen vehicle lifts, and even had a night shift that worked only on Smith Chevrolet inventory. They worked on customers' cars by day, and the dealership's cars by night.

This helped them to where they now had a great turn rate. Getting newly purchased vehicles onto the lot and retail-ready was happening quickly, and their customers were getting serviced quickly as well.

Despite all of that though, Alfred just knew that each tech could turn one more hour per day, couldn't they? There was always more there, there.

Every department could be a little more efficient. Every team member could perform 1% better. Every leader could care just a little more. Every lost deal could've been put together. Opportunities for growth were everywhere.

Alfred knew it and no matter how many people praised him and his team for all their success, he couldn't see them as anything more than C+ students, himself included. They were doing better than most, but still significantly less than their potential.

Alfred went back to the chest:

Title X

- CERTIFICATE OF TITLE NUMBER X -

A TEAM THAT READS TOGETHER
LEADS TOGETHER

HEAR ME, YOU EAGER SEEKERS OF WISDOM, FOR WITHIN THIS TITLE LIES A PRINCIPLE OF UTMOST IMPORTANCE: "A TEAM THAT READS TOGETHER LEADS TOGETHER." IN THE SACRED INTERPLAY OF INK AND PARCHMENT, IN THE SILENT HARMONY OF WORDS THAT CRAFT NARRATIVES AND THEORIES, TRUTHS AND TALES, RESIDES THE COLLECTIVE ENLIGHTENMENT OF MINDS AND SPIRITS UNITED BY COMMON OBJECTIVES.

LET ME ACKNOWLEDGE, AS THE DAWN OF UNDERSTANDING GRACES MY CONSCIOUSNESS, THAT THE TOME IN MY HANDS IS NOT MERE PAPER AND INK, BUT A VESSEL OF KNOWLEDGE, A CUP OVERFLOWING WITH THE NECTAR OF INSIGHTS GARNERED FROM MINDS BOTH ANCIENT AND CONTEMPORARY, NEAR AND FAR, RENOWNED AND OBSCURE.

AS I OPEN A VOLUME, MAY THE SYMPHONY OF IDEAS FLOW THROUGH THE SACRED STILLNESS, CASCADING INTO THE RIVERS OF MY CONSCIOUSNESS, NURTURING THE FERTILE GROUNDS OF MY INTELLECT WITH THE WISDOM OF SAGES, THE DISCOVERIES OF SCIENTISTS, THE MUSINGS OF PHILOSOPHERS, AND THE NARRATIVES OF STORYTELLERS WHO HAVE GRACED THE STAGE OF LIFE.

HOWEVER, THE ABUNDANCE HARVESTED FROM THESE FERTILE FIELDS IS NOT MINE TO HOARD BUT TO SHARE WITH MY COMRADES, MY COLLEAGUES, MY FELLOW TRAVELERS ON THIS JOURNEY TOWARDS MASTERY AND SUCCESS. THE ILLUMINATION THAT BATHES MY UNDERSTANDING IN ITS RADIANT GLOW IS MEANT TO BE A GUIDING LIGHT FOR ALL, ILLUMINATING THE PATH FOR EACH MEMBER OF OUR SACRED ASSEMBLY.

"A TEAM THAT READS TOGETHER LEADS TOGETHER." LET THESE WORDS RESONATE THROUGH THE HALLS OF OUR COLLABORATIVE ENDEAVORS, CARRYING THE PROMISE OF SHARED ENLIGHTENMENT AND COLLECTIVE EMPOWERMENT. MAY EACH TOME WE EXPLORE TOGETHER SERVE AS A BRICK, A BUILDING BLOCK IN THE CONSTRUCTION OF OUR UNITED WISDOM, A STRONGHOLD OF INSIGHT THAT STANDS IMPERVIOUS AGAINST THE FLOODS OF IGNORANCE AND MYOPIA.

AS WE DELVE INTO THE PAGES, MAY THE TAPESTRY OF KNOWLEDGE UNFURL BEFORE OUR EYES, ITS THREADS WEAVING THROUGH THE CANVAS OF OUR SHARED COMPREHENSION, CRAFTING A MASTERPIECE OF INTELLECTUAL AND SPIRITUAL WEALTH THAT BENEFITS NOT ONLY THE INDIVIDUAL BUT THE COLLECTIVE, THE TEAM, THE FAMILY WE HAVE FORGED THROUGH SHARED TOIL AND SHARED TRIUMPHS.

EVERY WORD, EVERY SENTENCE, EVERY PARAGRAPH WE CONSUME AND CONTEMPLATE TOGETHER BECOMES THE VIGOR AND MUSCLE, THE BONE AND TENDON OF OUR COLLECTIVE STRENGTH. OUR DISCUSSIONS, OUR DEBATES, OUR REFLECTIONS ON THE WRITTEN WORD SERVE AS EXERCISE, TRAINING THAT FORTIFIES OUR INTELLECTUAL PROWESS, RENDERING US FIT AND PREPARED FOR THE CHALLENGES AND OPPORTUNITIES THAT AWAIT.

WITH EACH BOOK WE COMPLETE, WITH EACH DISCUSSION WE ENGAGE IN, MAY THE BONDS OF UNDERSTANDING DEEPEN, MAY THE BRIDGE OF SHARED KNOWLEDGE STRENGTHEN, MAY THE TIES OF MUTUAL RESPECT AND ADMIRATION TIGHTEN. IN THE CRUCIBLE OF SHARED LEARNING, WE FASHION A TOOL MOST POTENT, A WEAPON MOST EFFECTIVE-AN OPEN, CRITICAL, REFLECTIVE, AND ENDLESSLY CURIOUS MIND.

LET THIS BE OUR MANTRA, OUR GUIDING STAR AS WE NAVIGATE THE SEAS OF ENTERPRISE AND INITIATIVE: "A TEAM THAT READS TOGETHER LEADS TOGETHER." IN THE SHARED PURSUIT OF KNOWLEDGE, IN THE COLLECTIVE QUEST FOR WISDOM, WE SHALL DISCOVER NOT JUST SUCCESS BUT SIGNIFICANCE, NOT JUST ACHIEVEMENT BUT FULFILLMENT, NOT JUST WEALTH BUT THE PRICELESS TREASURE OF ENLIGHTENED MINDS WORKING HARMONIOUSLY TOWARD A GRAND VISION AND A SPLENDID DESTINY.

The Title Marked X

A Team That Reads Together Leads Together

Hear me, you eager seekers of wisdom, for within this title lies a principle of utmost importance: "A Team That Reads Together Leads Together." In the sacred interplay of ink and parchment, in the silent harmony of words that craft narratives and theories, truths and tales, resides the collective enlightenment of minds and spirits united by common objectives.

Let me acknowledge, as the dawn of understanding graces my consciousness, that the tome in my hands is not mere paper and ink, but a vessel of knowledge, a cup overflowing with the nectar of insights garnered from minds both ancient and contemporary, near, and far, renowned, and obscure.

As I open a volume, may the symphony of ideas flow through the sacred stillness, cascading into the rivers of my consciousness, nurturing the fertile grounds of my intellect with the wisdom of sages, the discoveries of scientists, the musings of philosophers, and the narratives of storytellers who have graced the stage of life.

However, the abundance harvested from these fertile fields is not mine to hoard but to share with my comrades, my colleagues, my fellow travelers on this journey towards mastery and success. The illumination that bathes my understanding in its radiant glow is meant to be a guiding light for all, illuminating the path for each member of our sacred assembly.

"A Team That Reads Together Leads Together." Let these words resonate through the halls of our collaborative endeavors, carrying the promise of shared enlightenment and collective empowerment. May each tome we explore together serve as a brick, a building block in the construction of our united wisdom, a stronghold of insight that stands impervious against the floods of ignorance and myopia.

As we delve into the pages, may the tapestry of knowledge unfurl before our eyes, its threads weaving through the canvas of our shared comprehension, crafting a masterpiece of intellectual and spiritual wealth that benefits not only the individual but the collective, the team, the family we have forged through shared toil and shared triumphs.

Every word, every sentence, every paragraph we consume and contemplate together becomes the vigor and muscle, the bone and tendon of our collective *strength. Our discussions, our debates, our reflections on the written word serve as exercise, training that fortifies our intellectual prowess, rendering us fit and prepared for the challenges and opportunities that await.*

With each book we complete, with each discussion we engage in, may the bonds of understanding deepen, may the bridge of shared knowledge strengthen, may the ties of mutual respect and admiration tighten. In the crucible of shared learning, we fashion a tool most potent, a weapon most effective—an open, critical, reflective, and endlessly curious mind.

Let this be our mantra, our guiding star as we navigate the seas of enterprise and initiative: "A Team That Reads Together Leads Together." In the shared pursuit of knowledge, in the collective quest for wisdom, we shall discover not just success but significance, not just achievement but fulfillment, not just wealth but the priceless treasure of enlightened minds working harmoniously toward a grand vision and a splendid destiny.

Alfred rubbed his eyes. Clearly, reading had not been his strong suit for years. Even in the midst of his excitement, his eyes were getting tired just reading the Titles themselves sometimes. The thought of reading books together with his team was hard to wrap his mind around, but Alfred then reminded himself that if he really wanted to institute continued growth and change in his business, it would require a change in his leadership.

Alfred thought further about how little reading he actually did. He, of course, had audiobooks that he would occasionally listen to in the mornings during his workouts or in the car on his way to work, but it was definitely not often enough to call it a habit.

He could admit that he would read automotive magazines occasionally to catch up on news and the latest trends, and of course he read all kinds of stuff on his cell phone…social media feeds, news updates, things like that, but in all honesty, that was about it.

How could he ask the team to read together if he himself didn't read often?

Alfred was suddenly reminded of the next Title. He pulled it out and read it intently.

Title XI

- CERTIFICATE OF TITLE NUMBER XI -

WALK THE WALK

WITH THE DAWN THAT BATHES THE SKY IN ITS GOLDEN EMBRACE, USHERING IN A DAY PREGNANT WITH POSSIBILITIES, I UNFURL THE TITLE MARKED ELEVEN, CARRYING THE PRINCIPLE: "WALK THE WALK." IN TRUTH, THESE ANCIENT, MURMURING PAGES IMPART THE WISDOM THAT WORDS, THOUGH DIPPED IN THE INK OF SINCERITY AND WOVEN WITH THREADS OF PROMISE, GAIN TRUE WEIGHT ONLY WHEN MATCHED BY THE RHYTHM OF ACTION.

ALLOW YOUR EYES TO FALL UPON YOUR REFLECTION, YOU WHO SEEK WISDOM AND PROGRESS. WHAT DO YOU SEE? ARE YOU A LIVING TESTAMENT TO YOUR SPOKEN VOWS, A MANIFESTATION OF YOUR PROCLAIMED PRINCIPLES? IS THE SILHOUETTE YOUR SHADOW CASTS UPON THE EARTH ONE OF INTEGRITY AND COMMITMENT?

"WALK THE WALK," MURMUR THE VOICES OF ANTIQUITY—A SYMPHONY ECHOING THROUGH THE WINDS OF TIME, ENVELOPING MY EARS WITH THE MELODY OF ACCOUNTABILITY AND ACTION. TO DECLARE IS BUT THE FIRST STEP, A SPARK SEEKING KINDLING. TO ACT, TO MOVE WITH PURPOSE AND DELIBERATION, TO TREAD THE PATH CARVED BY YOUR WORDS—THIS IS THE FIRE THAT ILLUMINATES, THE FLAME THAT WARMS AND TRANSFORMS.

THROUGH THE DAYS' CORRIDORS AND THE NIGHTS' GALLERIES, LET MY FOOTSTEPS RESOUND WITH THE CADENCE OF MY WORDS. LET EACH STRIDE BEAR WITNESS TO MY COMMITMENTS, EACH MOVEMENT A DANCE OF PROMISES FULFILLED, AND EXPECTATIONS MET. IN LIFE'S SILENT THEATER, LET MY ACTIONS BE THE SCRIPT, MY DEEDS THE DIALOGUE, MY CHOICES THE UNFOLDING PLOT, AN INEVITABILITY OF TRUTH REALIZED.

AS I TREAD UPON LIFE'S STAGE, MAY THE WORLD'S AUDIENCE BEHOLD AN UNFEIGNED PERFORMANCE, A PLAY WHERE PROCLAMATIONS AND DEEDS DANCE IN HARMONY, INTERTWINED IN THE CHOREOGRAPHY OF SINCERITY AND PURPOSE. "WALK THE WALK," THE CHANT REVERBERATES—A CALL TO ARMS FOR THE SOUL THAT ASPIRES NOT ONLY TO DECLARE BUT TO DEMONSTRATE, NOT MERELY TO PROMISE BUT TO PROVE.

WITH THE MANTLE OF THIS SACRED PRINCIPLE UPON MY SHOULDERS, I VENTURE INTO THE DAY'S TAPESTRY, WEAVING THROUGH ITS HOURS WITH THE THREAD OF ACTION ALIGNED WITH PROCLAMATION. IN LIFE'S GRAND MARKETPLACE, LET MY CURRENCY BE NOT JUST WORDS, BUT DEEDS THAT PURCHASE THE RESPECT OF PEERS, THE TRUST OF PARTNERS, THE LOYALTY OF SUBORDINATES, AND THE LEGACY THAT REVERBERATES THROUGH THE ANNALS OF TIME.

I SHALL "WALK THE WALK" WITH STEADFAST AND PURPOSEFUL STRIDES, MOVEMENTS MIRRORING THE SYMPHONY OF MY DECLARATIONS. THROUGH MY COMMUNION WITH THIS SACRED TITLE, LET THE PRINCIPLE SEEP INTO MY MUSCLES, FLOW THROUGH MY VEINS, AND BECOME THE LIFE FORCE ANIMATING MY ACTIONS, INFUSING EACH CHOICE AND STEP WITH THE POWER OF INTEGRITY AND THE MAGNETISM OF AUTHENTICITY.

AS THIS TITLE IS SEALED, AS THE DAWN YIELDS TO THE DAY, I STEP FORWARD AS A WANDERER ARMED WITH THE COMPASS OF TRUTH, A TRAVELER GUIDED BY THE MAP OF SINCERITY. "WALK THE WALK," THE WHISPER CRESCENDOS INTO A ROAR, THE MURMUR TRANSFORMS INTO A CHANT, PROPELLING ME FORWARD AND ONWARD TOWARD THE HORIZON WHERE WORDS AND DEEDS CONVERGE, WHERE PROMISES AND ACTIONS EMBRACE, BENEATH A SKY PAINTED WITH THE HUES OF TRUST EARNED AND RESPECT GARNERED. IN THE SACRED DANCE OF DOING AND DECLARING, IN THE HALLOWED CONFLUENCE OF SAYING AND STEPPING, I DISCOVER THE MELODY OF SUCCESS, THE HARMONY OF PROGRESS, AND THE RHYTHM OF A LIFE WELL-LIVED.

The Title Marked XI

"Walk the Walk"

With the dawn that bathes the sky in its golden embrace, ushering in a day pregnant with possibilities, I unfurl the Title Marked Eleven, carrying the principle: *"Walk the Walk."* In truth, these ancient, murmuring pages impart the wisdom that words, though dipped in the ink of sincerity and woven with threads of promise, gain true weight only when matched by the rhythm of action.

Allow your eyes to fall upon your reflection, you who seek wisdom and progress. What do you see? Are you a living testament to your spoken vows, a manifestation of your proclaimed principles? Is the silhouette your shadow casts upon the earth one of integrity and commitment?

"Walk the Walk," murmur the voices of antiquity—a symphony echoing through the winds of time, enveloping my ears with the melody of accountability and action. To declare is but the first step, a spark seeking kindling. To act, to move with purpose and deliberation, to tread the path carved by your words—this is the fire that illuminates, the flame that warms and transforms.

Through the days' corridors and the nights' galleries, let my footsteps resound with the cadence of my words. Let each stride bear witness to my commitments, each movement a dance of promises fulfilled, and expectations met. In life's silent theater, let my actions be the script, my deeds the dialogue, my choices the unfolding plot, an inevitability of truth realized.

As I tread upon life's stage, may the world's audience behold an unfeigned performance, a play where proclamations and deeds dance in harmony, intertwined in the choreography of sincerity and purpose. *"Walk the Walk,"* the chant reverberates—a call to arms for the soul that aspires not only to declare but to demonstrate, not merely to promise but to prove.

With the mantle of this sacred principle upon my shoulders, I venture into the day's tapestry, weaving through its hours with the thread of action aligned with proclamation. In life's grand marketplace, let my currency be not just words, but *deeds that purchase the respect of peers, the trust of partners, the loyalty of subordinates, and the legacy that reverberates through the annals of time.*

I shall "Walk the Walk" with steadfast and purposeful strides, movements mirroring the symphony of my declarations. Through my communion with this sacred title, let the principle seep into my muscles, flow through my veins, and become the life force animating my actions, infusing each choice and step with the power of integrity and the magnetism of authenticity.

As this Title is sealed, as the dawn yields to the day, step forward as a wanderer armed with the compass of truth, a traveler guided by the map of sincerity. "Walk the Walk," the whisper crescendos into a roar, the murmur transforms into a chant, propelling me forward and onward toward the horizon where words and deeds converge, where promises and actions embrace, beneath a sky painted with the hues of trust earned and respect garnered. In the sacred dance of doing and declaring, in the hallowed confluence of saying and stepping, I discover the melody of success, the harmony of progress, and the rhythm of a life well-lived.

Alfred got the answer to his question.

How could ask his team to read together when he barely read anything himself?

The answer was, he couldn't.

"Allow your eyes to fall upon your reflection, you who seek wisdom and progress. What do you see? Are you a living testament to your spoken vows, a manifestation of your proclaimed principles? Is the silhouette your shadow casts upon the earth one of integrity and commitment?"

This paragraph in the Title was quite the smack in the face. He immediately thought about the people he admired and looked up to. All of them "Walked the Walk." It was the fact that they lived out their life's principles that attracted Alfred to them. From his pastor to his mentors, to guys like Grant Cardone, and Martin Luther King, Jr. Each one of them was predictable in the sense that you always knew what you were going to get.

Alfred guessed that if you asked his team, or even his family, they would tell you he was quite unpredictable. Sometimes he was on fire, other times he was barely smoldering. Sometimes he was the guy you could count on, other times he would let you down.

If Alfred wanted to establish a culture where his team would read books together and share their individual and collective wisdom, it was going to have to start at the top. Alfred had to learn to love to read. Knowing now what he knew about how it takes sixty-seven days before something becomes easier to do than to not do, Alfred committed to a minimum of eighteen minutes of reading per day, every day, for at least the next sixty-seven days.

Why eighteen minutes? A few years back Alfred had seen a video where billionaire Jesse Itzler talked about the fact that if you committed eighteen minutes a day to developing any skill, after one year you would be better than 95% of the population in that skill.

So, he decided he would attach reading to his daily morning routine. He would start listening to strictly audio books every morning. No music. No podcasts. Just books. He would start with one that he thought he'd really enjoy, figuring that would help make the transition from music and podcasts to audio books a little easier.

The next morning, he followed through on his commitment. He downloaded Matthew McConaughey's book, Green Lights because it seemed like a perfect place to start, and it absolutely was.

Read by Matthew McConaughey himself, the whole thing was like listening to one of the longest and best movies you've ever seen. It was amazing, and Alfred really got a lot from it.

Next, he went to Will Smith's book, Will, and it too was read by the author, Will Smith, himself. Between his voice, and the acting, and the singing, and the music, and the stories, it was a fun and insightful experience.

It wasn't long before Alfred not only picked up a habit of listening to audiobooks, but he also started having a tough time NOT listening to audiobooks. During his workout, in the car, anytime he would travel, audiobooks became something Alfred just couldn't get enough of.

He listened to *How to Win Friends and Influence People*, *Think and Grow Rich*, *Rich Dad Poor Dad*, *The Alchemist*, *Outwitting the Devil*, and a handful of others. Each "read" gave him so many ideas and inevitably propelled him to want to pick up another one. Over time, Alfred got to a point where he genuinely loved reading. Whether it was listening to an audiobook or holding a good old-fashioned, hardcover copy in his hands, Alfred now loved to read.

With that being the case, he knew he could now ask the rest of the team to join him, because a team that reads together leads together.

The lead part was something Alfred was chasing. He didn't always understand why he was so competitive, but when he would see that he was second place in his twenty group, or that they had finished third in the region, it would really get under his skin.

Just one time in his life Alfred wanted to be number one.

In order to take first, Alfred and his team were going to have to take the lead over all of their competition, and in order to take the lead over their competition, according to the Titles, they needed to read together.

Alfred sat down with his leadership team. He knew this would be the place where he needed to start. If he could get them to create the habit of reading, then it would be easier for the idea of reading together to trickle down through the culture of the whole store.

He bought them all a copy of The Five Dysfunctions of a Team and got them all to agree to read for at least eighteen minutes a day, every day. Then once a week, in their team leadership meeting, he would discuss with them what they'd learned so far, some of their takeaways, and how they could apply those in the dealership.

It started off slow. Many members of the team appreciated Alfred's enthusiasm, but just didn't quite understand why they were doing this. They'd gone their whole lives avoiding reading at all costs. At school, at home, everywhere.

Watching videos, or listening to podcasts, these things they could maybe stand behind, but books…ugh. They hadn't opened a book since high school and rarely opened them then.

Alfred didn't back down, though. He reminded them daily to read for eighteen minutes. He quizzed them sporadically in the halls as they passed on the contents of the book. There were even multiple times where they would happen to be in the restroom at the same time and Alfred would ask them to recite insights from the book while literally taking a pee.

It no longer mattered to Alfred. He had seen the power of applying the Titles and believed in them with everything in his being. Plus, now that he had broken through his own resistance to reading, and was "Walking the Walk," he was able to speak to the team and say things like: "I understand." ""Yup, I wasn't a reader either." "Believe me, I'm with you!" and because he could relate, he was able to inspire, motivate, and most importantly, activate his leaders.

They began reading together consistently, and when they finished one book, Alfred would immediately introduce another. There were books on leadership, books on building culture, books that were fun and entertaining like *Will and Greenlights* and books that were challenging to read like *The Blue Ocean Strategy and The Hero's Journey*.

Amazingly though, just as he had hoped, as the team read books together, gained insight and wisdom together, and deepened their bonds with one another, it started to trickle down. Alfred would walk into a daily morning meeting and see his leaders talking to their teams about the books they were reading. They would have slides up on the screen with relevant excerpts from the books, and many times Alfred would find out they bought copies of the books for the people they were leading.

The entire sales team ultimately became a team that reads together, and in time…well…

Alfred was sitting in his office when he got the call. It was 2:10 p.m. on a Wednesday afternoon. The phone said Garret Devorski. Garrett was the head of dealer relations at General Motors. He was an incredible guy, worked directly at headquarters, and him and Alfred had met a few times before at different dealer events in Vegas, golf outings in Virginia, and a handful of places in between.

"Good afternoon Mr. Devorksi." Alfred answered the phone joyfully.

"Afternoon Alfred. How's Betty? How are the kids?" Garret's voice confidently came through the line.

"Everyone is amazing sir." Alfred responded, taken aback by the fact that Mr. Devorski could manage to remember his wife's name even though he'd never met her. "Appreciate you asking. How can I best serve you today, sir?"

"Alfred, I wanted to call and congratulate you. Smith Chevrolet has just been named Chevrolet Dealer of the Year! Way to go Alfred! What you and your team have managed to do in the last five years is beyond anything I've ever seen, and I've been with General Motors for over thirty years. It truly has been remarkable to witness. You've managed to grow in volume, maintain a high customer satisfaction index, and now have outsold your market, your zone, and your region. It is an honor, sir, to be the one to be able to make this call. Out of everyone I know, you might be the one who I believe deserves this award the most. You have become quite an inspiration to dealers across the country Alfred. Congratulations, sir."

Alfred was smiling ear to ear. He, just like everyone else on his team, enjoyed a little encouragement every now and again, and this one here, coming from *The* Garret Divorski was one Alfred knew he would treasure for a lifetime.

"Thank you, Garret, truly sir, the honor is all mine. We couldn't have done it without the support from you and General Motors." Alfred and Garret talked back and forth for a few minutes before Alfred hung up the phone and let out a high-pitched yelp. "Whoo hoo!" He was on cloud nine. "Chevy Dealer of the Year!" he shouted. "No freaking way! Let's go!" As he fist-pumped the air, he could feel his heart beating powerfully in his chest. It was rapid and strong.

It was rhythmic and, at that moment, he felt more alive than he had since he was a kid.

This was what he needed. This is what everyone needed. By choosing to walk the walk, and developing a team that reads together, Alfred had taken his already successful team/work family to an entirely new level of success. They were Chevy Dealer of the Year now… and there was no looking back. The bar had been raised, and Alfred was determined to continue leaping over it.

CHAPTER 18
HERE WE GO AGAIN

> *"Your journey to greatness begins not by going elsewhere but by diving deep within, for it's in the depths of your own being that you'll discover the hero you were always meant to be."*
> **—Anonymous**

Alfred opened the door to his Midnight Edition Chevy Silverado for the thousandth time, a ritual that marked the beginning of another day in his life as the owner of Smith Chevrolet.

The birds greeted him with their melodic chirping as the sun's rays painted the eastern horizon with hues of orange and pink. There was a peculiar mix of sensations in the air; slight chill lingering from the fading summer, intermingled with the warm, stale embrace of the season's final days.

He climbed into the driver's seat and started the engine. The low growl of the truck was music to his ears, a familiar soundtrack to his daily commute. A faint cloud of exhaust swirled around his Maryland dealer plate, a symbol of the dealership that had been a part of his family for generations. Alfred's phone was in hand, and with a tap, he connected to the Bluetooth system. The soothing notes of the Bose stereo filled the cab with sound as he prepared for the twenty-three-minute journey ahead.

It was September 1st, a new day, a new month. August had drawn to a close on a positive note for Smith Chevrolet. They had managed to sell 531 cars, yielding a record amount of profit. The entire team was riding a wave of enthusiasm as they embraced autumn. It had been an amazing year in so many respects, and their effort had propelled them to first position in their zone, a top-10 ranking in the region, and the number one spot within their twenty-group. For a dealership with a sixty-year legacy, they were not only holding their ground, but what they were doing was extraordinary!

Alfred shifted his truck into drive, beginning his daily commute past rows of average-sized homes, their driveways filled with an array of different vehicles, each representing a slice of the automotive market. There were Ford Focuses, Kia Sorentos, Nissan Titans, and Toyota Tacomas, all within a few blocks of Alfred's home. A vivid silver Chevy Camaro occupied the corner house, while the cul-de-sac around the corner had a fleet of full-sized SUVs.

Every automotive brand seemed to have its presence in this neighborhood, and Alfred was absolutely stoked about that. After all, Smith Chevrolet was more than just one of the top one hundred Chevrolet dealerships in America; they also sold a wide range of used cars. What Alfred loved most, however, was the presence of his dealership's license plate frames on many of these vehicles.

A common game Alfred played no matter where he was traveling, was to look at the license plate frames of all the cars on the road. This would tell him who the biggest dealerships were in the area. The more license plate frames, the more successful that dealership was. It was a quick and straightforward way to gauge who was winning in the area, and who wasn't.

"Smith Chevrolet" license plate frames...had fortunately become an incredibly common sight on the roads.

As Alfred patiently waited at a traffic light, his attention was drawn to the Tesla Model 3 directly in front of him. The license plate frame read, *"Drive with History – Drive with Smith Chevrolet."* Smith Chevrolet was now notorious in the region for its relentless desire to offer customers an incredible experience, while moving the community forward, and developing the people in their ranks.

Alfred's mind drifted back to the days of old, when Smith Chevrolet license plate frames were everywhere. In those days you couldn't drive a block without encountering the iconic silver and blue frames that proudly displayed the Smith name.

And now the same could be said again, but with even far more reaching success than the company had ever seen before.

The traffic light turned green, snapping Alfred out of his trance. Just as he was about to accelerate, he got a notification on his phone. Glancing down briefly, he noticed it was an email from Garrett Divorski, the General Motors CEO. It was hopefully an announcement that they had won Dealer of the Year again, and Alfred had recently become a bit curious about whether they'd made the cut. For the moment, he decided to ignore the message and continue his journey.

As he merged onto the highway, Alfred took a deep breath, grateful for the season he and his family had been growing through "August was a ridiculously good month." He shouted to himself.

Coming in just a bit later than years past, thanks to most of the team leaders really stepping up, Alfred knew he would be walking in the dealership with radiant energy and celebration. He was feeling really good about things.

The noise of cars zooming past, semi-trucks shifting gears, and motorcycles weaving in and out of traffic somehow became oddly exciting for Alfred. Amidst the chaos, he thought to himself, "Opportunity is everywhere. Everyone buys a car."

Through the highway's constant movement, something familiar caught his eye—a massive billboard against the backdrop of the clear blue sky. It highlighted a sleek car with the tagline: "*Drive with History. Drive with Smith Chevrolet.*" It was a newer advertisement, perhaps from a month ago, and the sight of the billboard brought a smile to Alfred's face.

In that moment, Alfred felt a surge of pride. And, as more vehicles passed him, that pride became joy. The cars might have been diverse in make and model, but their license plate frames told a consistent story—one where Smith Chevrolet played an increasingly impactful role.

Alfred and his team…or should we say…" family," had grown from fifty people to now over 150 people.

Sales were strong month in, and month out, and between all the social media posts documenting the successes they'd had, there was a pipeline full of applicants wanting to work at Smith Chevrolet. Next to that pipeline, was an additional one full of customers that couldn't wait to do business with Smith Chevrolet.

Today was one of those days where it all felt too good to be true, but then Alfred reminded himself that both he and all team members had put in the work to get here. It's not like the Titles popped up and magically everything changed. No. They had invested five years of commitment to "The Morning 5".

Five years, every single day, having powerful morning meetings that followed the L.E.A.D.D. process. Five years of learning, growing, and applying the principles of the Titles, reading together, creating a calendar so he could become a servant leader, walking the walk, promoting from within.

Alfred and his team had clawed tooth and nail to get where they were, and Alfred, at the very least, was committed to keep growing.

Not for his success, but for the opportunity to create success for others.

He went to his office, opened the safe, and grabbed the chest. There was one Title left to implement.

Title XII

- CERTIFICATE OF TITLE NUMBER XII -

TRAIN YOUR PEOPLE ON LIFE SKILLS
NOT JUST JOB SKILLS

UPON UNROLLING THE TITLE MARKED XII, WE ENCOUNTER A PRINCIPLE OF PROFOUND IMPORT: "TRAIN ON LIFE SKILLS, NOT JUST JOB SKILLS." LIFE SKILLS ARE THE THREADS THAT WEAVE THEMSELVES INTO THE VERY FABRIC OF OUR CHARACTER, FORTIFYING US TO NAVIGATE THE TURBULENT WATERS OF EXISTENCE WITH GRACE AND SAGACITY.

JOB SKILLS, LIKE FLEETING SHADOWS, ARE TRANSIENT AND EVANESCENT, SHIFTING WITH EACH DAWN OF TECHNOLOGY AND INNOVATION. IN CONTRAST, LIFE SKILLS ARE THE ENDURING PILLARS, UNWAVERING THROUGH THE PASSAGE OF TIME, BESTOWING UPON US A REPOSITORY OF KNOWLEDGE AND WISDOM.

WE MUST NOT WAVER IN OUR COMMITMENT TO PRIORITIZE THE IMPARTING OF THESE ESSENTIAL LIFE SKILLS. TAKE HEED, FOR WEALTH MANAGEMENT STANDS AS ONE OF THESE INVALUABLE TREASURES. TO GRASP THE SUBTLE ARTS OF SAVING, INVESTING, AND NURTURING WEALTH IS NOT MERELY A PATH TO FINANCIAL LIBERATION, BUT A VEHICLE FERRYING US TOWARD A LIFE REPLETE WITH CHOICES AND POSSIBILITIES.

RELATIONSHIPS, DELICATE AND PRECIOUS, SERVE AS THE LIFEBLOOD OF OUR HUMAN JOURNEY. HENCE, WE MUST EQUIP OURSELVES WITH THE ABILITIES TO NURTURE AND SUSTAIN THESE BONDS. EFFECTIVE COMMUNICATION, PROFOUND EMPATHY, AND A DEDICATION TO COMPREHENDING THE HEARTS AND MINDS OF OUR FELLOW TRAVELERS ARE INDISPENSABLE IN THE CRAFTING OF RELATIONSHIPS THAT OFFER BOTH JOY AND SUPPORT.

INDEED, COMMUNICATION IS A REVERED ART, A HARMONIOUS DANCE OF EXPRESSION AND RECEPTION. BEYOND THE MERE EXCHANGE OF WORDS, IT INVOLVES RECOGNIZING UNSEEN EMOTIONS, RESPONDING GENTLY TO UNSPOKEN NEEDS, AND THOUGHTFULLY RESPECTING THE SHARED SPACE WE OCCUPY WITH OTHERS.

LET US NOT CONFINE OUR VISION. AS MENTORS AND GUIDES IN THIS GRAND TAPESTRY OF EXISTENCE, LET US BROADEN OUR HORIZONS TO ENCOMPASS THE CULTIVATION OF LIFE SKILLS. THESE SKILLS EMPOWER INDIVIDUALS NOT ONLY TO TRAVERSE THEIR PROFESSIONAL TERRAIN BUT ALSO TO REVEL IN A LIFE ENRICHED WITH UNDERSTANDING AND CONNECTION.

LET US EMPOWER INDIVIDUALS WITH CRITICAL-THINKING, PROBLEM-SOLVING, AND THE INNOVATIVE SPIRIT NECESSARY TO NAVIGATE LIFE'S INTRICATE TAPESTRY WITH DISCERNMENT AND CREATIVITY.

THEREFORE, LET OUR MISSION BE UNEQUIVOCAL. OUR FOCUS SHOULD NOT BE CONFINED TO THE ACQUISITION OF MERE JOB SKILLS, BUT INSTEAD, IT SHOULD ENCOMPASS THE EXPANSIVE PANORAMA OF LIFE'S POTENTIAL. LET US FOSTER A HOLISTIC APPROACH TO DEVELOPMENT, WHERE INDIVIDUALS ARE NOT ONLY PROFICIENT IN THEIR VOCATIONS BUT ENLIGHTENED IN THE ART OF LIVING.

WITH THE WISDOM FROM TITLE MARKED XII AS OUR GUIDING LIGHT, LET US COMMIT TO NOT ONLY TRAINING FOR TASKS BUT EDUCATING FOR LIFE. LET US IMPART KNOWLEDGE AND WISDOM THAT ILLUMINATE THE PATH TO A LIFE OF SUBSTANCE, JOY, AND UNPARALLELED FULFILLMENT.

The Title Marked XII

Train Your People on Life Skills, not Just Job Skills

Upon unrolling the Title Marked XII, you encounter a principle of profound import: "Train on Life Skills, Not Just Job Skills." Life Skills are the threads that weave themselves into the very fabric of our character, fortifying us to navigate the turbulent waters of existence with grace and sagacity.

Job skills, like fleeting shadows, are transient and evanescent, shifting with each dawn of technology and innovation. In contrast, life skills are the enduring pillars, unwavering through the passage of time, bestowing upon us a repository of knowledge and wisdom.

I will not waver in my commitment to prioritize the imparting of these essential life skills. Take heed, for wealth management stands as one of these invaluable treasures. To grasp the subtle arts of saving, investing, and nurturing wealth is not merely a path to financial liberation, but a vehicle ferrying me toward a life replete with choices and possibilities.

Relationships, delicate and precious, serve as the lifeblood of our human journey. Hence, I must equip myself with the ability to nurture and sustain these bonds. Effective communication, profound empathy, and a dedication to comprehending the hearts and minds of my fellow travelers are indispensable in the crafting of relationships that offer both joy and support.

Indeed, communication is a revered art, a harmonious dance of expression and reception. Beyond the mere exchange of words, it involves recognizing unseen emotions, responding gently to unspoken needs, and thoughtfully respecting the shared space I occupy with others.

Let us not confine our vision. As mentors and guides in this grand tapestry of existence, let us broaden our horizons to encompass the cultivation of life skills. These skills empower individuals not only to traverse their professional terrain but also to revel in a life enriched with understanding and connection.

Empower individuals with critical-thinking, problem-solving, and the innovative spirit necessary to navigate life's intricate tapestry with discernment and creativity.

Therefore, my mission will be unequivocal. My focus will not be confined to the acquisition of mere job skills, but instead, it will encompass the expansive panorama of life's potential. I will foster a holistic approach to development, where individuals are not only proficient in their vocations but enlightened in the art of living.

With the wisdom from Title Marked XII as my guiding light, I commit to not only training for tasks but educating for life. Imparting knowledge and wisdom that illuminates the path to a life of substance, joy, and unparalleled fulfillment.

Alfred stared at the timeworn car title in his hands. He had read the Title Marked Twelve dozens of times over the years; more times than any of the others. Each time he read it, he was reminded of the old proverb: "Give a man a fish, he eats for the day; teach a man to fish and he eats for a lifetime." But this time it felt different.

He could only imagine what his life would've been like if all those years he'd spent in the car business, someone would have taught him things like wealth-management, relationship-building, communication skills, business acumen, parenting, etc. These things were never taught in automotive. In fact, if you looked from the outside, you would think the opposite was being taught. The industry was known for promiscuity, money wasting, divorce, estranged children, unprofessionalism, and the list goes on and on.

This was what the Title was alluding to, and this was the concept that intrigued Alfred the most. He wanted his life to matter. For him, it had always been about something more than just selling cars and running a business. Alfred wanted to make a multi-generational impact. He wanted not just to make a difference in one person's life, but ultimately to make an impact on their entire family tree.

He wanted to be able to shift the trajectory of the single mom who had come from an extensive line of near poverty, and questionable influence; or the young kid that no one else would give a chance, due to the cultural way he looks, walks, talks; the background he had established. Alfred had been born into opportunity, and for his entire life he never went without. Though for many this can be a curse, for Alfred it inspired an intense amount of both gratitude and responsibility that fueled him to want to truly help others make their mark in the world.

And now in his hands, Alfred had a roadmap of exactly how to do so.

"We will teach them all to fish," he said to himself, and then… in an instant…he realized he already had.

By executing the previous eleven Titles Alfred had created a culture of growth and development that anyone could step into. With the right amount of desire and work ethic, they could completely change their lives, and the lives of all those in their blood line that came after them.

Morning Routines, Goal Setting, Career Development, Success Formulas, Relationship Skills, Communication and Collaboration, Service to Others, Humility and Positivity, The Value of Good Character, The Importance of Education and Constant Growth, Setting the Example and Walking in Excellence; all of this and more was being taught at Smith Chevrolet every single day.

Alfred had transformed the dealership from a business that sells cars, to a business that develops people.

The cars they sold, the profits they made, the success of the business, it all was simply a byproduct of being of service to his people. They grew, and so, naturally the business did as well. The traditional business concept had been turned upside down.

Instead of focusing on profits, customers, and then employees, Alfred had been focusing on employees, which in turn led to more customers, which of course led to more profits.

"You're driving with history, yeah, you're driving with history. You're driving with history, at Smith Chev-ro-let," popped into Alfred's mind.

History.

His-tory.

His Story.

Alfred stared at the chest as the memories of the day he received it came flooding back. He missed his grandfather deeply, and at the same time he was incredibly grateful for the gift he'd left behind.

12 Titles. 12 Principles. Infinite impact.

With the Titles in hand Alfred was creating a legacy that he knew would long out live him. Just as the Titles had promised.

In his moment of reflection, he decided to flip through each Title, summarizing their contents into a cheat sheet he could always carry with him.

1. **The Morning 5 – Arise Early and Be a Creator:** Get up early and start your day with purpose. It's all about taking control of your morning and setting yourself up for a successful day.

2. **Focus on Your Business Goals, Not Those Set by Others:** Stick to your own business goals, don't get sidetracked by what others think you should achieve. It's your path, own it!

3. **Promote from Within:** Look around you; the best people for higher roles might already be part of your team. Growing your own talent is key.

4. **The 8-5-3-1 Formula:** This is a strategy for making the most out of leads and turning them into sales. It's about being efficient, and focused, in your sales approach.

5. **Make People Feel Special, Important, and Like They're the Only One:** Treat every person like they're your most important one. It's all about making personal connections that last.

6. **Build a Family:** Create a work environment that feels like a family. When everyone feels valued and part of the team, amazing things happen.

7. **Be A Servant Leader:** Lead by helping others. It's about putting your team first and showing the way by your own actions.

8. **Carry an Attitude of Gratitude:** Be thankful for the good things and people in your life. A little gratitude goes a long way in business and life.

9. **Hire and Fire on Character, Not Credentials:** Choose (and let go of) people based on who they are, not just what's on their resume. Integrity and character matter most.

10. **A Team That Reads Together Leads Together:** Encourage your team to read and learn together. Sharing knowledge helps everyone grow and brings the team closer.

11. **Walk the Walk:** Don't just talk a good game – make sure you're living out your promises and values in real, tangible ways.

12. **Train Your People on Life Skills, Not Just Job Skills:** Train your team skills that go beyond the job – like how to communicate well, manage finances, and think critically. It's about preparing them for life, not just work.

Alfred folded the notebook paper and put it in his wallet. He vowed to carry it with him every day and refer to it regularly. The Legacy Titles had been the greatest gift he'd ever been given, and he looked forward to the day that he too could pass them on to the next generation, leaving a Legacy of impact for many years to come.

EPILOGUE

Hello.

I hope you've enjoyed the story of Alfred and Smith Chevrolet. You'll be pleased to know that if I were to continue the story Alfred would go on to not only become the second largest used car franchise dealership in the United States of America, but he would have dozens of months where he sold over 800 cars a month, and even one month in March of 2018 where he sold 1,132 cars.

"Hogwash!" you'd say. "Impossible." "It's just a made-up story!"

And in some respects, you would be accurate. Alfred is a fictional character. Completely made up in my mind. Smith Chevrolet never existed, it's not real, I made it up too.

However, the story itself.... His-Story...It's real.

I had the honor of being the General Manager at Dan Cummins Chevrolet in Paris, Ky. With incredible tutelage from the owners of the dealership, Josh Cummins, and Dusty Cummins, we were able to grow the dealership 800% in just under six years. From 131 cars a month, to over 800 cars a month, with one incredible experience in March of 2018 where we sold 1,132 cars in twenty-seven business days, while closed on Sundays.

We did so with a team of forty-three salespeople, twelve front line sales reps (aka BDC), seven finance managers, four desk managers, one general sales manager, the "Triplets," and me, Glenn Lundy, General Manager.

We had daily morning meetings.

We stood and shouted, "I am on a mission to eradicate the negative stigmas associated with the car business. I will make people feel special, feel important, and like they're the only one. I will offer an experience that will exceed my customers' expectations today, tomorrow, and in the future. I will not just sell cars; I will create fans.," every single morning.

We paid attention to license plate frames and read books together.

We hired inexperienced people with great character and developed them into leaders.

We promoted from within.

We led each day with gratitude and attacked The Morning 5.

We generated eight leads per day, per salesperson, and had a team of people all selling twenty or more cars per month.

In fact, they still do.

We applied the four "P"s of social media, and even live-streamed all of our Saturday morning sales meetings. (Feel free to look them up on Facebook, just search for "Glenn Lundy Dan Cummins.")

We did all the things in this book that, if you've read this far, you are now privy to.

I…We…Lived the story of Alfred Smith.

I left Dan Cummins years ago, and to this day, they not only still operate at that level, but they've also expanded into two additional dealerships and now sell over 1,500 cars a month between the three stores.

But it's not about the cars.

It was never about cars.

It was always about His-Story.

The literal thousands of men and women that were shifted, impacted, and positively influenced by the development of their character, and the implementation of the twelve Titles above.

So yes, Alfred Smith is not real. But His-Story, is.

And if you choose, His-Story can become your story, too.

JOIN THE COMMUNITY...

Thank You for Embarking on This Journey! As you close the final chapter of "The Legacy Titles - A Parable for Success - 12 Proven Principles to Grow Your Business 800%", we want to express our heartfelt gratitude for joining us on this transformative journey. But remember, your journey doesn't have to end here. It's time to take the inspiration you've gained and turn it into action!

Welcome to the Morning 5 Community.

We are excited to offer you an exclusive opportunity to become part of a vibrant, supportive community dedicated to continuous growth and success. The "Morning 5" Community is a hub of learning and inspiration, where you can:

- Access a plethora of self-development courses.

- Learn the intricacies of podcast creation.

- Dive into the world of real estate investment.

- Explore a wide range of topics to enrich both your personal and professional life.

All This for Just $17 a Month!

For just $17 a month, you can unlock a treasure trove of knowledge and join a community of like-minded individuals all striving towards betterment and success.

READY TO RISE AND GRIND?

Morning 5 Community

Scan the QR code below to learn more about the RiseandGrind University and the Morning 5 Community and to begin your membership. This is more than just a subscription; it's an investment in yourself and your future.

Don't let the momentum stop now. Harness the energy, insights, and inspiration you've gained from the book and channel it into continued learning and growth. We can't wait to welcome you to our community where every day is an opportunity to rise, grind, and shine!

Printed in the USA
CPSIA information can be obtained
at www.ICGtesting.com
JSHW072307250124
55896JS00006B/8